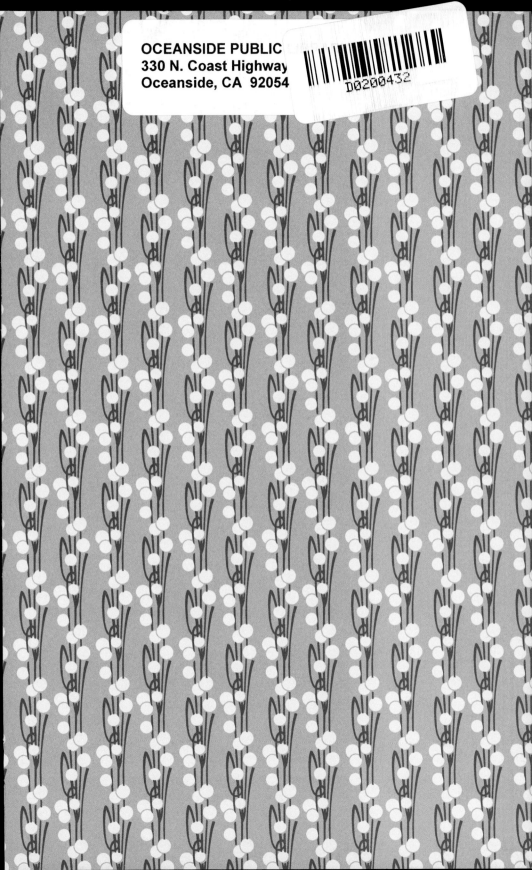

75 Remarkable Fruits
for Your Garden

75 Remarkable Fruits
for Your Garden

Jack Staub

ILLUSTRATIONS BY
Ellen Sheppard Buchert

Gibbs Smith, Publisher
TO ENRICH AND INSPIRE HUMANKIND
Salt Lake City | *Charleston* | *Santa Fe* | *Santa Barbara*

First Edition

11 10 09 08 07   5 4 3 2 1

PUBLISHED BY
Gibbs Smith, Publisher
PO Box 667
Layton, Utah 84041

ORDERS: 1.800.748.5439
www.gibbs-smith.com

DESIGNED BY Kurt Wahlner and Steve Rachwal
PRINTED AND BOUND in Hong Kong

Signed prints of the artwork in this book are available from the artist,
Ellen Sheppard Buchert, by contacting her at ellenbuchert@yahoo.com

Library of Congress Cataloging-in-Publication Data

Staub, Jack
75 remarkable fruits for your garden / Jack Staub ; illustrations by
Ellen Buchert.— 1st ed.
p. cm.
ISBN 13: 978-1-4236-0250-7
ISBN 10: 1-4236-0250-1

Dedication

To my sisters Sharon Staub Doty,
Nancy Peck Staub Laughlin, and Harriet Staub Huston,
and my brothers Dr. Charles Lincoln Hussey Staub
and Nicholas Edwards Staub, who are ample proof that,
while the apple may not fall far from the tree,
there can be wild variations in form and flavor.

❧ Contents ❧

❦ Introduction ❦

This volume has been as much a learning curve for me as, hopefully, it will be for you, and I willingly admit that I have only personally cultured perhaps a score of the fruits in this book and that, prior to beginning my research, I had never even heard of some of them. That said, I have been tireless in my quest for the most accurate and up-to-date information, the most intriguing facts and historical illuminations, and the best of the current batch of available cultivars in every case. I have researched and "googled" deeply, checking and cross-checking facts, ferreting out dates and sources, exposing inaccuracies, swimming through the intricacies of non-compatible information, and wrestling out-and-out contradiction to the ground. Therefore, far from being an expert, I hope you will view me as your ruthless and dedicated conduit for all this information: streamlining, poking and prodding, and holding every particle of it up to the brightest light of day, until I have rendered it brief, accurate, and hopefully literate and amusing in the bargain. To the very best of my knowledge and capabilities, what I set before you is both horticultural and historic fact.

Let me be candid: the culture of fruit plants is far more daunting than that of the vegetables with which I am well acquainted, as, for one thing, most are stubbornly perennial rather than annual, and there are the particulars of fertility and pollination, as well as temporal and climatic considerations to take into account. For instance, for some of these fruit types, varieties that will do well on the West Coast or in the North of the United States are completely inappropriate for culture in the East or South. When I have run into this dilemma, I have tried to recommend one for each coast or climate. And when I have chanced upon a fruit plant that is self unfertile and will need an alternate pollinator, meaning that you will have to plant at least two or three varieties to achieve fruit, I have noted these specifics as well. Additionally, you will find that, in many cases, I have made the culinary recommendation, due to the natively astringent and seedy personality of some berries in particular, to render them into a kind of all-purpose juice or nectar through a process of boiling or steaming, then mashing, sieving, and sweetening. Do try to look beyond the somewhat tedious nature of this processing to the superlative health benefits most of these berries bring to the table: they far outweigh this slight gastronomic hardship. And finally, if I have discovered that culture of any of the fruits in question is simply too much of a trial, but acquaintance with the fruit or fruit product is desirable, I have made that eminently clear as well.

Generally, I have eschewed plants that are, zonally, severely limited, particularly to our warmer zones, although, in some chapters, I have been moved to recommend dwarfed varieties of interesting tropical or subtropical fruit plants for pot culture so as to make them available to the greatest number of you. And in other cases, I have lumped together two or three or more cultivars in a single chapter (particularly the rash of modern *Rubus* and *Prunus* hybrids) as, in my educated analysis, they are basically variations on a limited theme and undeserving of a solo turn in the sun. My greatest joy in this tome was to introduce to both myself and you the fruit plants of incredible but mainly obscure health potential, principally in the area of antioxidancy. Cultivars like the wolfberry, jujube, goumi, magnolia vine, and sea buckthorn are worthy of universal attention and I am thrilled to be able to extol their virtues here.

I have included a brief bibliography at the back of this book but would like to extend my thanks here to some of the sources I found invaluable. These include Lee Reich's wonderful book *Uncommon Fruits For Every Garden*, the historic *Herballs* of everyone from Theophrastus and Pliny the Elder to John Parkinson, Nicholas Culpeper, and John Gerard, Web sites like *Dave's Garden*, *Ty Ty Nursery*, *The Wiccan Herbal Encyclopedia*, *Botanical.com*, *Bible Gateway.com*, a whole slew of University Web sites (Illinois, New Jersey, Oregon, Virginia, Washington), the very helpful folks at Monticello, the University of Hawaii Department of Agriculture, Cornell University's Geneva Station, Gary Mount of Terhune Orchards in Princeton, New Jersey, and, most of all, my staunch ally, the *Wikipedia*, without which the accuracy and depth of this tome would have been impossible. I will close in adding that, while many of the fruit plants described here within may be novel to all of us, I have a hefty list of really remarkable cultivars for which I will be finding some space in the new fruit border I have dancing in my head. My fervent hope is that you will be equally inspired.

Jack Staub
Hortulus Farm
Wrightstown, PA

❧ 1. Apple 'Ashmead's Kernel' ❧
2. Apple 'Celestia'
Malus domestica

The apple tree is so anciently regarded that, in British lore, "Avalon,"
where King Arthur was taken to die, translates to "Isle of Apples,"
and the Greek "Elysium," where the worthy were destined to spend
their afterlives, to "Apple Land."

As we all know from that familiar Garden of Eden scenario
(although is was probably an apricot that actually done the
dirty deed), the apple is many millennia old, apple seeds having
been found in Stone Age settlements in Switzerland dating to 8000 B.C.
The tart, wild crab apple (*Pyrus malus*), native to the Caucasus and
Turkey, is thought to be the ancient ancestor of the lot, and the first trees
to produce our familiar sweet apple are believed to have grown near the
modern city of Alma-Ata, Kazakhstan. Belonging to the greater *Rosaceae*
clan, the cultivated apple, *Malus domestica*, has most probably been
under global culture since the dawn of nearly any civilization you can
name, Alexander the Great having been known to have imported dwarf
apple types into Greece from Asia Minor in 300 B.C. Apple trees were so
important to the early Celts that to chop one down was punishable by
death, a seventh-century Celtic poem proclaiming "three unbreathing
things paid for only with breathing things: an apple tree, a hazel bush, a
sacred grove."

Along with their cousin the pear, apples are known botanically as
"pomes," from the Latin *Pomona*, sharing the characteristics of a paperlike
central core, crisp flesh around the core, and a thin outer skin.
Interestingly, the apple has stood for immortality, as in the precious apples
doled out to the gods by the Nordic goddess Iduna to keep them forever
young, and, exactly the opposite, for the earthly cycle of birth, death, and
rebirth. Pomona, alternately known as the "Apple Mother," was the
ancient Roman goddess of fertility and fruition, and also represented the

APPLE 'ASHMEAD'S KERNEL'

apple's antique association with the great yearly cycle, this mandala-like imagery stemming from the apple's ostensible resemblance to the sun: born each day in pink, apple-blossom clouds, and then ripening from yellow to red as it crosses the sky, ultimately to "drop" as if from a tree into the west. In Baltic lore, for example, the Sun Goddess made this daily journey in a flashing, copper-wheeled chariot, headed for her apple orchard home beyond the western horizon.

Probably the most famous allusion to the apple in all of mythology concerns the deific competition it provoked amongst the powerful goddesses Athena, Hera, and Aphrodite. It seems that Peleus, the son of Aeacus, king of Aegina, was marrying the water nymph Thetis, and *tout* Olympia was invited, save for Eris, the goddess of discord, which is certainly understandable. Eris, however, took umbrage, arrived uninvited, and, for pure provocation, rolled a golden apple inscribed *kallisti*, or "for the fairest," at the feet of Hera, Athena, and Aphrodite. Naturally, this attractive bauble was claimed by each of the goddesses at hand, so it fell to Paris, prince of Troy, to decide which of them should snare the prize. As true to things political today as it was then, each of the interested parties offered Paris a substantial bribe, Hera offering him wisdom and power, Athena heroism and victory, and Aphrodite the most beautiful woman in the world, Helen of Troy. Paris, who clearly should have opted for the wisdom, took the beauty instead, Aphrodite got the crown, and the Trojan War was effectively begun.

Apples were first delivered to North America with Columbus in 1493, and records from the Massachusetts Bay Company indicate that apples were being grown in New England as early as 1630. Surely our most venerated American apple grower must be the folk hero John Chapman of Leominster, Massachusetts, better known as "Johnny Appleseed." Living off the land and in harmony with all God's creatures during the first half of the nineteenth century, Johnny Appleseed founded countless orchards throughout Pennsylvania, Ohio, Michigan, Indiana, and Illinois. Today, in part thanks to John Chapman, there are more than 7,000 varieties of apples grown in the U.S., although mostly in home gardens as a scant 20 varieties comprise more than 90 percent of our commercial apple industry. With so many varieties from which to choose, the best that can be done in this volume is to introduce you to a couple of historic superstars: the ancient English variety 'Ashmead's Kernel,' and the ambrosial American heirloom 'Celestia.'

First planted by a Dr. Ashmead in Gloucestershire, England, before 1720, the "exquisitely homely" 'Ashmead's Kernel' is flattish and of an unassuming russet hue splashed with orange or red. However, its crisp yellow flesh is consistently triumphant in blind taste tests against far flashier varieties, the English writer Philip Morton Shand speaking of its "honeyed nuttiness" and opining "no apple of greater distinction or more perfect balance can ever have been raised anywhere on earth." This reigning English darling was introduced into the U.S. in the 1950s by pomologist Robert Nitschke and is surely worth a patch of ground in any garden.

The American heirloom apple 'Celestia' was first mentioned in U.S. horticulturist John Aston Warder's *American Pomology—Apples 1887.* Warder gave "best" ratings to a number of historic favorites like the 'Esopus Spitzenberg' and 'Newtown Pippin,' Thomas Jefferson's and George Washington's favorites respectively, but he reserved the "very best" crown for 'Celestia' alone, lauding its "profusely aromatic and spicy flavor." In 1869, A. J. Downing, America's most prominent nineteenth-century arbiter of taste, proclaimed that 'Celestia' was "crisp, tender, juicy" and "very pleasant." Then, shortly after the turn of the twentieth century, without so much as a "by your leave," 'Celestia' vanished from view until it was triumphantly rediscovered by fruit explorer Conrad Gemmer of Susquehanna, Pennsylvania, in an orchard in New Jersey in 1996. The unostentatious exterior of 'Celestia', with pale green skin often mottled with a pink or brownish blush and speckled with very fine spots, encloses a lusciously complex flesh so legendary, it is still proclaimed one of the most delicious apples in existence.

Apples can be tricky in terms of procreation, as a seed from a chosen variety cannot be trusted to replicate its parent. Therefore, apple trees are generally created by grafting "scions" or apple buds, which will grow true to species, onto accommodating rootstock. As well, all apple trees need cross-pollination to fruit successfully, so it will be necessary to companion plant an 'Ashmead's Kernel' or 'Celestia' with another type that

Apple 'Celestia'

blossoms at the same time to ensure optimal yield. That said, apples are generally hearty and uncomplaining creatures, although they will grow best where winter temperatures hover near freezing for at least two months of the year, and one should take care to prune young trees during their formative years so that their branches are equally distributed. An apple tree will begin to bear fruit 6 to 8 years from planting, but is then capable of producing fruit for up to an astonishing 100 years, which is a lot of applesauce. And that would be the perfect thing to do with either of these lovely specimens.

3. Apricot 'Blenheim'
4. Apricot 'Rival'
Prunus armeniaca

It is believed by a host of ethno-botanists and mythologists that the legendary "nectar of the gods," the beverage of choice on Mount Olympus much noted for its honeyed sweetness, was, in fact, the juice of the apricot.

Although the apricot's Latin designation *armeniaca* would lead one to believe that Armenia was its ancient point of origin, it is, in fact, northeastern China that botanists have identified as this sunny, sweet-fleshed fruit's birthplace, most placing the date at about 1000 B.C. A *Prunus* member of the greater rose family and cousin to the plum, peach, cherry, and almond, the apricot subsequently spread throughout Asia, ultimately wending its way into Armenia by about 300 B.C. It is believed by some to have been introduced into the Mediterranean basin by no less than Alexander the Great in the fourth century B.C., upon his return from China. In ancient Persia, the apricot was reverentially referred to as "the egg of the sun," and in Turkey, Iran, Iraq, Afghanistan, Pakistan, and Syria, where the apricot flourishes, it is equally respectfully called "the moon of the faithful." Apricots, however, appear to be a far-flung and generally unsociable family, as every region of every country in which the apricot thrives seems to have it own signature cultivar virtually unknown to the rest of the world. For most of history, people seemed to have been content with whatever local variety sprouted, for, unlike most other edible plant families, little selection seems to have taken place anywhere within the apricot genus until the nineteenth century.

The word "apricock" first appeared in English print in 1551, deriving from the Latin *praecoquus,* also the root for the English word "precocious" and, in this case, meaning "early ripening." Symbolically, the apricot, along with the peach and other stone fruits, and certainly

APRICOT 'BLENHEIM'

because of that suggestive, slightly fuzzy cleft these *Prunus* cousins share, was an ancient icon of female genitalia; in medieval France, for instance, the word *abricot* was a popular slang term for "vulva." It is probable some apricots made their way across the Atlantic to the eastern coast of the Americas with the earliest settlers, but it was the Franciscan missionaries, who made their way into California in the late eighteenth century, who really got the apricot rolling in North America, and it was in the area south of San Francisco in 1792 that the first major U.S. production of apricots was recorded. Here, however, is where we come up against a somewhat cheerless truth: 95 percent of U.S.-grown apricots still come from California, with apricot orchards covering an impressive 21,000 acres of Californian land. "Why?" you may ask, and with good reason. To lunge straight for the heart of it, the apricot is a fruit plant that carries with it a tiresome propensity to swooning attacks if the temperatures and climatic conditions are not wholly agreeable, causing some to simply throw a wooly shawl at the tedious thing and cry "have done with it!" For instance, apricots are keen on lots of moisture but not soggy feet, seem to prefer a cool, foggy summer and a damp, warm one equally, and can be broadly subject to loss of bloom or fruit by spring frost, while at the same moment requiring an adequately cold winter dormancy. California seems to have exactly the right conditions for apricot growing, although, as I have mentioned, what they are exactly is hard to pin down. "Difficult," as one would refer to a testy relative, I think about sums it up.

That said, the 'Blenheim' and 'Rival' apricot types would be an excellent place to try your luck, 'Blenheim' being one of our two biggest commercial varieties and as widely accommodating an apricot personality as you will meet, and 'Rival' being a late-twentieth-century hybrid famous for its adaptability as well as its superior and luscious yields. Named for the seat of the dukes of Marlborough in Oxfordshire, and also known as 'Royal Blenheim,' 'Blenheim' is an English heirloom dating to about 1850, and comprises nearly 30 percent of California-grown apricots. 'Blenheim' blooms relatively late so that danger of blossom loss due to frost is happily mitigated, is self-fruitful so no cross-pollination is necessary, and will harvest toward the end of July in most regions. The fruit of the 'Blenheim' is a rich, golden yellow with a rosy blush, and the flesh firm, juicy, and delightfully aromatic, with an excellent balance of sugar and acid.

First bred by Dr. Thomas K. Toyama of the Washington State University Research Foundation, 'Rival' is famous for its adaptability as well as for its superior yields of really enchanting fruit. This late-twentieth-century hybrid's amber fruits are winningly blushed with a glossy red over a good bit of their surface, and most boast a few red freckles, too. The firm flesh is slightly dry on the apricot scale, but intensely aromatic and faintly tart, and an average yield can be as much as 70 pounds per tree. Bloom time is midseason, which means it will miss most frosts as well. The one slight glitch in the mainly laudable performance of the 'Rival' is that, while most U.S.-grown cultivars are self-fruitful, 'Rival' is not, so you will need to plant an alternate apricot cultivar that blooms at the same time as 'Rival' ('Riland' or 'Perfection' are likely candidates) in order to achieve fruit.

Medicinally, apricot seeds were used to treat tumors in an astonishingly early 502 A.D., and, in Great Britain, apricot oil was used as an erstwhile cure for tumors and ulcers throughout the seventeenth century. Interestingly, the contemporary drug Laetrile, a currently controversial cancer therapy, is derived from an extract of apricot seeds. Champions of this treatment believe that, as the apricot pit extract breaks down, it releases cyanogenic glycosides when it comes into contact with a specific tumor-produced enzyme, thereby preferentially killing cancer cells at tumor sites. Modern medicine also confirms that apricots are an excellent source of beta-carotene (one apricot will provide you with 10 percent of your daily recommended amount), vitamin C, iron, potassium, and fiber.

Both 'Blenheim' and 'Rival' produce truly lovely trees: small to medium-sized with a dense spreading canopy, glossy reddish-brown bark, pretty heart-shaped leaves, and positive flurries of pretty white *Prunus* blossoms. Although it can take 4 years for a young tree to begin fruiting, once established, a single tree can bear as much as 45 pounds of apricots a year for 20 years or more. Culturally, despite their need for regular waterings, try to keep in mind the finicky apricot's aversion to wet feet: if your soil is of the heavy clay variety, dig in some rubble before planting. Also, for optimal fruit size and harvest, you may want to thin

APRICOT 'RIVAL'

your fruits to every 2 to 4 inches per branch, this best done right after flowering. Our Viennese friends ply us with mouth-watering apricot dumplings in season, wrapped in phyllo dough parcels and drenched in butter with a sprinkling of sugar, so here let me stop to recommend that sumptuous recipe to you. Try to make two your limit.

5. Blackberry
'Oregon Cutleaf Thornless'
✥ 6. Blackberry 'Triple Crown Thornless' ✥
Rubus laciniatus, Rubus fruticosus

"I'll stain your fingers and your face,
And then I'll laugh at your disgrace.
But when the bramble-jelly's made,
You'll find your trouble well repaid."

—Cicely Mary Barker (1895–1973)
"The Song of the Blackberry Queen"

The vast *Rubus fruticosus* clan, including as it does blackberries, raspberries, and all their bastard progeny, also comprises one of the most bewilderingly diverse plant families in the world. Botanists still cannot decide whether there was a single original blackberry that gave birth to the current baffling array of global relations, or, in fact, every sector of the globe gave birth to its own brood of favorite sons and daughters. The blackberry's native distribution ranges from the frozen tundra of the Arctic to the most sweltering of tropical climes, on every continent save Antarctica, and in Europe and Asia there are over 2,000 named varieties and 66 separate species and, in England alone, 41 known species. In fact, blackberries are so weedily invasive in so many parts of the globe that many intelligent individuals would positively snort at the suggestion that one might choose to plant one, and in Australia and New Zealand, where they were introduced in the nineteenth century, they are so truly invasive that New Zealanders wryly comment that there are only two types of blackberries currently growing there: one garroting the south, the other suffocating the north. It seems that they will grow on any site of former human habitation, taking root apparently to the depths of hell, and extending their thorny yet winningly berry-laden canes skyward.

Members of the greater *Rosaceae* family, blackberries have been known antiquely by many names, including "brambleberry" and "brumblekite," derived from the Old English *brymbyl* for "prickly." They have been consumed in England since Neolithic times, and were also so generally employed as a thorny, marauder-dissuading hedgerow that John Gerard commented in his *Herball* of 1636: "the bramble groweth for the most part in every hedge and bush." The "bramble," in fact, was so universally and antiquely in evidence that it was elevated to parable status in the Bible (Judges 9:7–15) in the story of Yotam, the true son of King Gid'on, and his struggle for the crown with his evil half-brother Avimelech, the lowly bramble commenting to the olive, the fig, and the grape vine: "If in truth you anoint me king over you, then come and take refuge in my shadow; and if not, then fire will issue from my roots and consume the cedars of Lebanon."

Throughout ancient Europe, it was believed that the color of the fruit was a result of the devil having either spat or urinated upon it, and that picking it after Michaelmas (October 11) would bring bad luck crashing about you, as the devil had once fallen into a thicket of blackberries and had left a curse on them. In Great Britain, it was also held that passing beneath an arch of brambles suckered into the earth at both ends could cure rheumatism, boils, whooping cough, blackheads, and fairly near anything else that happened to plague you, and a decoction of blackberry leaves was recommended as a remedy for both ulcers and venomous bites. In 1636, John Gerard herbally lauds them as a valuable astringent, serving to "heal the eies that hang out," and also notes that "the leaves of the bramble boiled in water with honey, alum, and a little white wine added there to" would "fastneth the teeth." As well, a popular early hair coloring was made by boiling blackberry leaves in lye, this apparently imparting to the hair a "soft black colour." On a more modern medical note, a handful of blackberries will give you 19 percent of your daily dose of vitamin C and is an excellent source of folate and vitamin E. Recent studies show that the anthocyanins in blackberries may reduce the risk of heart disease and inhibit colon cancer.

The two varieties I will commend to you here, one a tried-and-true heirloom and one a happy modern hybrid, will give you all this and more.

Blackberry 'Oregon Cutleaf Thornless'

BLACKBERRY 'TRIPLE CROWN THORNLESS'

The Oregon Cutleaf blackberry is an English native, apparently carried from Walton Heath in Surrey to the South Seas by an English settler, and then purportedly delivered into Oregon by a Frenchman in about 1850. Known in Great Britain as the "Evergreen Black," "Cutleaf," or "Parsley-Leaved" blackberry, the Oregon Cutleaf is known not only for its well-flavored, glossy black fruit, but also for its extreme vigor and productivity. As well, it is one of the blackberry varieties that will produce fruit and seed without fertilization, so you will need no cross-pollination. The 'Oregon Cutleaf Thornless,' which I enthusiastically recommend here, and which was born spontaneously in the Oregon wild in 1930, boasts the same winning attributes with the added luster of being entirely pain-free to harvest. As anyone who has ever wrestled with a blackberry bush knows, this must certainly constitute a point of near miraculousness.

The aptly named modern hybrid 'Triple Crown Thornless' is everything a blackberry could hope to be, boasting the triple threats of flavor, productivity, and vigor, and also managing to throw in disease resistance, immense fruit size, and, yes, *mirabile dictu,* thornlessness in the bargain. 'Triple Crown Thornless' was first developed in 1986 at the U.S. Agricultural Research Service's fruit laboratory in Beltsville, Maryland, and finally released to the public in 1996. Suitable to every venue from berry farms to home gardens, 'Triple Crown Thornless,' which will ripen anywhere from mid-July to mid-August, will ensure a mouth-watering midsummer supply of immense, glossy black, highly flavorful berries. In Oregon trials, Triple Crown plants have been known to yield an impressive 30 pounds or more of berries per plant, tests also indicating that 'Triple Crown Thornless' is well-adapted to nearly all American climate zones (5–8).

With their brambly, weedy reputation, it should be apparent that, once planted, you can fairly kick sand in a blackberry's face and it will respond by flourishing and fruiting without so much as a wince. An eye to pruning and some staking will be all that is required: like all *Rubus* species, blackberries are perennials that produce on one- and two-year-old "canes," the first year canes (*primocanes*) growing without flowering, the second year canes (*floracanes*) flowering, fruiting, and expiring with an exhausted sigh. Therefore, in the fall, remove expired *floracanes* canes or, alternately, prune back the entire stand to 12 inches immediately following harvest so that some *primocane* growth will occur before frost to fruit the following year. And speaking of "exhausted sighs," let us recollect here that blackberry wines and cordials have provided man with an excellent pick-me-up across countless centuries and cultures, so why not give this ancient *receipte* a try? Crush a big pot of blackberries, adding one quart of boiling water for each gallon of fruit, and allow to stand for a day; strain off the solids, add 2 pounds of sugar for every gallon of liquid, pour the result into a becoming vessel, and keep tightly corked. A year hence, let the games begin!

❧ 7. Blood Banana ❧
Musa acuminata 'zebrina'

*The term "Banana Republic" was coined in the nineteenth century
when American Minor Keith began growing bananas in Costa Rica
and, with the help of the occasional well-timed U.S. invasion, ultimately founded the United Fruit Company and came to literally own
entire Central American governments.*

Bananas have provided man with nutritious lunch-box fare since
prior to recorded history, and many horticulturists believe the
banana may well have constituted the earth's first fruit. Closely
related to the tropical ornamental plants *Heliconia*, bird-of-paradise
(*Strelitzia*), and the traveler's palm (*Ravenala madagascarensi*), bananas
are members of the *Musaceae* family, and most botanists cite the jungles
of Malaysia as their probable birthplace. The general supposition is that
they were then spread to the Pacific Islands and Hawaii by the accommodating early Filipinos, although Hawaiian legend maintains that it was a
brother of the fire goddess Pele who first carried *mai'a* to Hawaii. The
first written account of the banana dates to a Buddhist text of 600 B.C.,
followed by a subsequent mention in Indian documents of the fourth
century B.C., and the first reference to organized banana culture dates to
a Chinese manuscript of 200 A.D. By 650 A.D., the banana had been
imported into Palestine and, finally, in the tenth century, along the spice
roads into Europe. It was the Spanish missionary Tomás de Berlanga who
carried the banana to the New World in 1516; however, their official
introduction to the North American public did not occur until 1876
when, at the Philadelphia Centennial Exhibition, the then-exotic banana
was offered to the delighted throng for the extravagant price of ten cents
a finger.

Contrary to popular misconception, bananas do not grow on "trees"
at all but rather, like their cousin lilies, orchids, and palms, are actually
classified as "herbs." These handsome giant "herbs" with their signature

massive leaves can tower to 20 feet or more, with multiple leaf stems bearing 10 to 14 banana "hands," each "hand" composed of 18 to 20 banana "fingers." Being tropical plants, bananas are clearly not appropriate for culture in any climate below USDA zone 8 with the exception of the dwarf varieties, which can be grown under glass in winter and set out in summer. Therefore, it is toward these I will happily direct you now. While both the Dwarf Cavendish banana, growing to 5 to 8 feet, and the Novak Super Dwarf, growing to only 5 or 6 feet, produce small, sweet fruit and are perfect for pot culture, here I choose to point you toward the gorgeous if somewhat culinarily suspect *Musa acuminata 'zebrina,'* or blood banana.

Native to India and Indonesia and growing to 6 to 9 feet, the blood banana is a truly spectacular plant most notable for its dramatic foliage, which is a rich wine red on the underside and mottled with deep crimson and bronze on the top. Consider the additional splendor of lavish clusters of yellow flowers with deep red-purple bracts and you've got a fruit plant to be reckoned with, indoors or out. Although there is some debate about the edible desirability of the blood banana's small 3- to 4-inch fruit, I contest they are worth growing for their visual glamour alone, the key ingredients for successful pot culture being good light, thorough watering, the occasional feeding, and, of course, protection from frost. Wheel the pot outdoors when temperatures are uniformly above 50 degrees and your blood banana should do splendidly. Bananas are an excellent source of vitamin C, potassium, and dietary fiber, have no fat or cholesterol, and are highly recommended for their famous replenishment of carbohydrates, glycogen, and body fluids. Therefore, whether or not it comes from your blood banana, I recommend packing a nice ripe one in your lunch box to unzip at a faltering moment.

Blood Banana

8. Blueberry 'Rubel'
❦ 9. Blueberry 'Sunſhine Blue' ❦
Vaccinium corymbosum

" *'Blueberries as big as the end of your thumb,*
Real sky-blue, and heavy, and ready to drum
In the cavernous pail of the first one to come!' "

—Robert Frost, "Blueberries," 1949

There are a good number of extremely early fruit plants, but many botanists believe a blueberry antecedent could be the most ancient living thing on earth, stepping up to the cereal bowl at a whopping 13,000 years old. There are *Vaccinium* varieties native to virtually everywhere, including Europe, Scandinavia, the Far and Middle East, and both Americas. Therefore, the extended blueberry family includes countless permutations on a theme, from the condensed and crawling to the vigorously upright, and every zone and climate has its own favored native son as well as a few eminently creditable modern cultivars selected and hybridized from the wild. So, while in this tome I will commend to you two wonderful cultivars suitable to many zones and climes, there are most certainly others of similar description that will serve you well should either fail to thrive for you. Every home deserves a blueberry bush.

As we have discussed, *Vacciniums,* also known historically as "bilberries," "whortleberries," and "hurtleberries," are a vast and global clan, although the true blueberry is actually native only to the Americas, the United States alone accounting for 90 percent of the world's commercial crop. However, every global corner has a close *Vaccinium* cousin of which to boast, John Gerard describing both a black and a red "wortle" in his *Herball* of 1636, noting that "they grow plentifully in both the Germanies, Bohemia, and in divers places of France and England," and further commenting that the black variety is "full of a pleasant and sweet juyce"

Blueberry 'Rubel'

which does "colour the mouth and lips of those that eat them." Legend has it that the very first batch of "blaeberry" jam was concocted in the early sixteenth century by the French chefs brought into Scotland by Mary of Guise, the French-born wife of James V and mother of the infamous Mary, Queen of Scots. More distant relations of the blueberry in the greater *Ericaceae* or heath family include a number of popular ornamental plants, most notably rhododendrons, azaleas, mountain laurels, and heathers.

Both Virgil and Pliny lauded the virtues of their native *Vaccinium*, and blueberries have certainly figured in the native diet of the Americas since prehistory, in 1615, Samuel de Champlain noting that the Indians of the Great Lakes region not only harvested but venerated the blueberry. Many Native American tribes, it seems, believed the "star berry" was a gift from the gods to be conserved and employed in times of famine, and that the five-pointed "star" at the blossom end of each berry was stamped there by the hand of the Great Spirit himself. Native Americans enjoyed this earthly bit of manna fresh, smoked, dried, and famously pounded into venison to make an early blueberry-scented jerky called *Sautauthig*. Curatively, they employed a strong decoction of the root to soothe the pangs of childbirth and blueberry leaf tea as a highly efficacious purifier of the blood.

To certainly oversimplify another miasmic exercise in global botany, there are three basic types of "true" blueberry, mainly grown on the American continent: Highbush (*Vaccinium corymbosum*), Lowbush (*Vaccinium angustifolium*), and Rabbiteye (*Vaccinium ashei*). As their names would suggest, "Highbush" are erect shrubs and "Lowbush" are trailing crawlers; "Rabbiteye," named for their beady berries, are also erect shrubs. Equally simplistically, each of these three "true" varieties is defined in part by its favored home, the main factor being each plant's seasonal requirement of cool dormancy (below 45 degrees). Therefore, in eastern North America, Lowbush types are adapted from Canada down through Maine, Highbush types from New England down through the Carolinas, and Rabbiteyes from the Carolinas down to Florida. Just to add to the confusion, while Northern Highbush plants are self-fruitful and need no pollinizer, although they will fruit better and larger if one is

BLUEBERRY 'SUNSHINE BLUE'

supplied, Rabbiteye cultivars are either partially or completely self-incompatible, and Lowbush types are totally self-incompatible and must have a pollinizer to set fruit.

Then, to confound things further, two new hybrids have recently leapt upon the *Vaccinium* scene: the first the 'Southern Highbush,' a cross between a Northern Highbush, a Rabbiteye, and an Evergreen blueberry (*V. darrowii*), and similar in many ways to a Northern Highbush, its greatest difference being its low chilling requirement, making it perfect for American Southeast culture. The second is the Half-High Highbush, a cross between a Northern Highbush and a Lowbush. The plants are also similar to the Highbush in fruit characteristics but exceedingly compact in habit at only 2 to 4 feet, and were bred to be adaptable to the extreme cold and heavy snowfalls of our most northerly states.

Therefore, here I will stop to recommend to you one stalwart heirloom variety of the Northern Highbush variety called 'Rubel,' as it is not only self-fruitful, but adaptable to USDA zones 4 through 7 as well, and the most noteworthy of all the new Southern Highbush hybrids, the blueberry 'Sunshine Blue,' called by some "the ultimate edible ornamental." 'Rubel' is one of the first blueberries ever selected from the wild by Dr. Frederick V. Coville and Elizabeth Coleman White for the Whitesbog Cranberry Plantation in Browns Mills, New Jersey. Named in 1912 for Rube Leek of Chatsworth, New Jersey, one of the "pineys" hired by Elizabeth White to search the New Jersey Pine Barrens for the best wild specimens, the strong, upright habit, admirable productivity, and ease of picking of the 'Rubel,' combined with its small, uniform, deep-midnight, sparklingly flavorful fruit, have made it a historic favorite with generations of growers. Additionally, while all blueberries are antioxidant powerhouses, 'Rubel' scores almost twice as high on antioxidant content as most others.

Movie-star gorgeous, the Southern Highbush 'Sunshine Blue' leads its list of sterling attributes with a rounded, almost boxwood-like, semi-dwarf habit of 3 to 4 feet, glossy semi-evergreen, silver-tinged leaves, extremely vivacious hot pink flowers instead of the general-issue white, and masses of sweet, fat, deep blue berries, most plants yielding up to 10 pounds per season. As well, the ravishing 'Sunshine Blue' is perfect for pot and patio culture, and is one of the easiest blueberries to grow, being more tolerant of an elevated pH, having an incredibly low chill requirement at only 6-plus days, yet also being hardy as far north as Chicago and Seattle (USDA zones 5 to 10). When 'Sunshine Blue' berries turn from green to pink and, finally, to that glorious, brilliant blue, they are ripe for the picking, although they will hold on the bush, actually continuing to sweeten, for a good time.

Blueberries, in general, will prefer a slightly acidic soil (pH 4.5 to 5.2), benefit from a nice dressing of organic matter, and will not tolerate nitrate nitrogen-based fertilizers, so head in the direction of one of the ammonium sulfate–based brands used for azaleas and rhododendrons. John Gerard observed in his *Herball*: "The people of Cheshire do eat blacke Wortles in cream and milk, as in these South parts we eat Strawberries," which sounds like a lovely idea.

10. Cherry 'Montmorency'
11. Cherry 'Rainier'
Prunus cerasus, Prunus avium

In a reversal of the typical journalistic "hatchet job," the tale of our first American president's inability to tell a lie is, in fact, a fabrication concocted by Parson Mason Locke Weems in his overly laudatory Washington biography of 1800.

Cherries are believed by most botanists to have originated in the area between the Black and Caspian seas in Asia Minor in about 4000 B.C., then entering the Middle East by the third millennium B.C., and, from there, many believe it was birds that carried cherry pits into Europe prior to even human civilization, *avium*, the sweet cherry's subgenus being Latin for "of" or "for the birds." The English word "cherry" originates in the Assyrian *karsu* and the Greek *kerasos*, which also gave birth to the sour cherry's current subgenus sobriquet *cerasus*. Cultivation probably began in Greece in about 300 B.C., Pliny the Elder reporting 8 different varieties being cultivated in Italy by the first century A.D., and also mentioning that they had spread into cultivation as far north as Great Britain by that same date. Then, bizarrely, during the Dark Ages, the art of their cultivation in northern Europe seems to have been misplaced altogether, and the cherry had to be entirely reintroduced into England in the sixteenth century by that famous gourmand Henry VIII. By 1640, however, more than two dozen cultivars were recorded there, many imported to the New World by the first Massachusetts Bay colonists in 1629.

As everyone who has ever lost theirs knows, the ancient cherry has traditionally been associated with virginity, a notion which undoubtedly arose from the intensely uterine symbolism of voluptuous crimson flesh enclosing a precious seed. There are two main types, the sweet cherry, *Prunus avium*, eaten right off the tree, and the sour or "tart" cherry, *Prunus cerasus*, which is used almost exclusively for pie filling. Upon their

Cherry 'Montmorency'

CHERRY 'RAINIER'

introduction into the New World, sour cherries seemed to do admirably, especially as they continued their journey westward to the middle of the continent, where French missionaries distributed seeds while they made their way to the Great Lakes in the late eighteenth century. But sweet cherries refused to prosper in the hot humidity of the eastern United States and did not find a truly accommodating home until they were delivered to the Pacific Northwest in the early nineteenth century. There they took to the cool, temperate climes like hand to glove, and, currently, Oregon and Washington are our heaviest producers, accounting for over 60 percent of the U.S. sweet cherry crop. There is bizarrely little crossover along this climatic Mason–Dixon line, so in this book, I have in egalitarian fashion elected to offer up one sweet cherry for the West, and one sour cherry for the East.

It was Peter Dougherty, a Presbyterian missionary, who planted the first sour cherry orchard in the rolling hills of the Old Mission Peninsula above Grand Traverse Bay, Michigan, in 1852, although the local Cadillac Indians were apparently less than enthusiastic about the chances of this provocative new import. Dougherty, however, persisted, and, by 1893, the first commercial Michigan cherry orchard, Ridgewood Farm, was planted a cherry pit's throw from Dougherty's original site. Today, Traverse City is known as the "Cherry Capital of the World," producing over 40 percent of the annual U.S. sour cherry crop. Sour cherry cultivars are divided into two main groups, the "Amarelles," identified by their vigorous, upright trees, pale or reddish fruit, and low acidity, and the "Morellos," characterized by small, bushy, compact trees, dark red fruit, and higher acidity. It is the Amarelle variety 'Montmorency,' however, that is universally judged to be the superstar of pies, jellies, and juices, accounting for a whopping 95 percent of all U.S. sour cherry production, and the one we will romance here. The fruit of the midsized 'Montmorency' is a deep yet bright red with clear, juicy flesh, and, aside from handily surviving the heat and damp of eastern U.S. summers, 'Montmorency,' like all sour cherries, is self-fruitful, bears later then the sweet types, which makes it infinitely more frost resistant, and is widely recognized for its excellent productivity.

The American sweet cherry industry was born in 1847, when

Henderson Lewelling planted an orchard in western Oregon with nursery stock he had laboriously transported by ox cart from Iowa, ultimately culturing America's most illustrious sweet cherry, the 'Bing,' which got its name from the stalwart Manchurian foreman of Henderson's brother Seth Lewelling, another well-known grower. Other important sweet cherry varieties include the 'Lambert,' which also got its start on the Lewelling farm, and the 'Rainier,' which, together with the 'Bing,' accounts for more than 95 percent of Northwest U.S. sweet cherry production, about half of which are sold for fresh consumption, with another 40 percent being sold as the "Maraschino" cherry, that bright, brined, lipstick-red thing that has decorated ice cream sundaes and smart cocktails since the dawn of both hotel bars and soda fountains. It is the 'Rainier' cherry—a truly gourmet cherry crossbred in 1952 from 'Bing' and 'Van' varieties by Dr. Harold W. Fogle of Washington State University—that we choose to enthuse about in this particular volume. The 'Rainier' is as fresh, bright, and voluptuous a cherry as you will ever encounter—exceptionally large with a sunny yellow skin blushed with a gorgeous pink/red. Interiorly, the 'Rainier' is equally attractive, with finely textured flesh and superbly sweet juice. As sweet cherries are self-incompatible, cross-pollination by a non-'Rainier' cherry will be essential, so you will need two or three cherry trees, which is a very pretty idea indeed.

Cherries are chockablock with nutrients, including the important antioxidants beta-carotene and quercetin, which also provides significant anti-inflammatory relief for gout sufferers, and pectin, that cholesterol-lowering soluble fiber, as well as impressive doses of vitamin C, sour cherries having almost double the amount as the sweet types. Additionally, it is really hard to beat a cherry tree in blossom, and these two are glorious trees with clouds of ethereal white blooms in spring. Therefore, why not give one (or two) a try. In general, it is wise to keep cherry trees pruned to about 12 feet for ease of picking, and spaced 20 to 30 feet apart for optimal sunlight and airflow. Excellent crops can be expected from both these cultivars after about 5 years, after which trees will remain happily productive for 25 years or more. The leaves, limbs, roots, and pits of all cherries contain high concentrations of cyanogenic glycoside and are extremely toxic, so please be forewarned. That said, in the case of the sweet 'Rainier,' I advise, particularly to those of you who suffer from gout, to grab a handful of cherries right off the tree and have at it. As for the 'Montmorency,' how about a basketful in a chilled summer soup? Boil a pitted pound of them in 1½ quarts water with ¾ cup granulated sugar till soft, stir in a mixture of a cup of sour cream leavened with a pinch of salt, a tablespoon of confectioner's sugar, and 2 tablespoons of flour; chill, adjust seasonings, and serve to sundry gasps of delight.

❧ 12. Chokeberry 'Autumn Magic' ❧
Aronia melanocarpa

"A wire broom upside
down. Chokeberry tree branches
sweep white falling crumbs."

—Maija Rhee Devine,
"Chokeberry Tree In Winter," December 2001

Despite the fact that the *Aronia* is an extremely decorative shrub anciently native to North America and bears fruit of a truly powerful antioxidancy, I would hazard to guess that most of you are totally unacquainted with it. In any case, this will be an excellent opportunity to learn a bit about an American native genus of many notable attributes, chokeberries actually being two varieties distinguished by fruit color in the vast *Rosaceae* family: the red chokeberry (*Aronia arbutifolia*) and the black chokeberry (*Aronia melanocarpa*). Both are native to eastern North America from northern Florida up to Nova Scotia and as far west as Indiana, and *Aronias* dotted the forests of the upper Green Bay of Wisconsin when St. Philippine Duchesne, the French-born founder of the first free school west of the Mississippi, made her journey to Wisconsin in 1840 to found a school for the noble Potawatomi tribe. We know that the Potawatomi steeped the black chokeberry, which they knew as *nîki'mînùn,* into a tisane for colds, and *Aronia* seemed to have generally been known as an edible and medicinal plant among the Northeast tribes, many employing it like the blueberry and cranberry in the manufacture of pemmican, but clearly the chokeberry has never achieved the same level of popularity.

There is a reason for this: the chokeberry is so notably astringent that even birds will "choke" on it, leaving it to grace the woodlands until finally sought out as a winter food of last resort. However, *Aronia* berries, particularly the black variety on which we will concentrate here, when

CHOKEBERRY 'AUTUMN MAGIC'

sweetened, are not only good, they are *unbelievably* good for you. In fact, studies in Japan, Poland, and the United States have shown that the black chokeberry, due to its deep, anthocyanin-rich hue, is so powerfully antioxidant that its health benefit potential could be staggering in the treatment of everything from circulatory and urinary tract problems to cancer, heart disease, and gastrointestinal issues. Additionally, other studies still under evaluation show potentially huge employment in the treatment of chronic inflammation and liver failure. Now factor in a midsized habit; small, pink-white, lightly fragrant flowers borne in clusters in spring; neat, glossy, ovate leaves turning to flame in fall; and blueberry-sized fruit hanging from red pedicles in pretty clusters that will turn from green to black as they mature.

The black chokeberry I have just described is 'Autumn Magic,' an ingénue on the *Aronia* stage, which seems to have supplanted the formerly favored German-bred darlings 'Viking' and 'Nero' for the virtues of smaller leaves, more intense foliage, and a tidier habit. Grown, tested, and introduced by the University of British Columbia Botanical Garden in Canada, 'Autumn Magic' will also set loads of excellent fruit and has truly brilliant orange/red autumn foliage. Like all chokeberries, 'Autumn Magic' will forgive almost any growing condition or soil, tolerating both wet and arid situations, acid through alkaline soil, and full sun or part shade. It seems untroubled by insects or disease and is hardy to USDA zone 4 at least. A single specimen would be superb in a shrub border, tucked behind some smaller shrubs as they can be a tiny bit "leggy," but 'Autumn Magic' would be equally effective massed as a clump or hedge, where the fall show of glossy black fruit against dazzling foliage might be enjoyed to particular advantage. You'll have to juice the fruit, either by steam extraction or the "mash and drip" method, the steam method producing about 2 cups of juice per pound of berries, with some feeling that freezing the berries before mashing releases more juice. Mix with a like amount of apple juice to sweeten, and tip down what must surely be a standard-setting "elixir of life."

❧ 13. Coralberry (Snowberry) ❧
Symphoricarpos orbiculatus

Thomas Jefferson was so taken with the Pacific Slope snowberry delivered to him by Lewis and Clark in 1806 that, after cultivating it at Monticello, he sent a token of cuttings to his Parisian paramour, la Comtesse de Tessé.

Although it is not my habit in this tome to recommend fruit plants that are essentially inedible, in the case of the beauteous *Symphoricarpos* family, I will make an exception. Also known colloquially as Indian currant, buckbush, devil's shoestring, buckberry, snapberry, waxberry, and wolfberry, the coralberry and snowberry are mainly differentiated by the color of their berries, the coralberry being a glossy purple to crimson or lilac and the snowberry being, as you might guess, a snowy white. Berry-wise, the honest truth about both coralberries and snowberries is that they are justifiably bitter and, if eaten in quantity, can cause vomiting and diarrhea. However, the Pacific Slope snowberry was a traditional food source for northwestern Native Americans, who ate them dried or preserved in bear grease, as well as employing them mashed into a paste as a poultice for smarting eyes and, alternately, as a shampoo. It is also known that northeastern Native American tribes employed the dried roots to "stun fish for collecting and eating." I can only guess that they must have thrown a lot of them awfully hard.

There are fewer than 20 species of *Symphoricarpos*, and all, save one, which is Chinese in origin, hail from North America. A member of the honeysuckle family and a cousin to both vibernums and weigelas, the coralberry is essentially native to eastern North America, while the snowberry is essentially native to the Northwest. In a typical botanical example of one man's meat being another's poison, coralberries are adored by a host of plantsmen for the winter interest of their vivid berries, while their wilder relations are regarded as a semi-invasive weed in some southeastern states.

CORALBERRY (SNOWBERRY)

One of the truly brilliant things about the greater American *Symphoricarpos* family, however, as one might guess from their semi-"weedy" reputation, is that they seem impervious to drought and frost (USDA zones 2 to 6), will do well in even the most recalcitrant soils, and withstand pollution like storm troopers, making them perfect for urban planting. Additionally, the taller members of the clan, with their handsome green foliage, will make a bang-up screening or informal hedge idea, while the shorter-growing relations are excellent for planting on erosion-prone banks, as their roots will bind and hold the soil. Although both coralberry and snowberry blossoms are small, ranging in tone from white to pink, both will flower with profusion in late summer, that pretty opening act introducing the main event of the fall/winter berry show, which will happily persist well into the frostiest snow-covered months.

A few of the more interesting cultivars are the dwarf hybrid Hancock coralberry (*Symphoricarpos* x *chenaultii* '*Hancock*'), a spreading shrub growing to only a foot and a half with bell-shaped, pink flowers and pink/coral berries in autumn; Thomas Jefferson's favored Pacific Slope snowberry (*Symphoricarpos albus* var. *laevigatus*), with a naturally compact and rounded habit, handsome foliage, pink to white blossoms, and fat, half-inch-in-diameter berries; and the 'Magic Berry' coralberry (*Symphoricarpos* x *doorenbosii* '*Magic Berry*'), with soft pink flowers, deep green foliage, and striking lilac-pink fruits that mature to a deep winey color, growing to about 4 feet tall and wide. The only trick to the *Symphoricarpos* family, as they are prone to "wandering" via stolons (which is why they make such fantastic hedges), is that some curtailment and pruning will be beneficial both to their shape and to their surrounding plantings. Both coralberries and snowberries are a superb food source for many wild animals and birds, so, despite their inadvisability for human consumption, why not view this chapter as a gastronomic exercise in giving a bit back?

❧ 14. Cornelian Cherry ❧
Cornus mas

Ancient Roman legend maintains that Romulus, when seeking to establish the city that would be Rome, hurled a spear from the Aventine hill, and where it struck the ground, a Cornelian cherry tree rose to mark the destined spot.

Far older than man and thought to be originally native to the region of the Black Sea, the Cornelian cherry, actually a type of dogwood, is believed to have arisen in Europe as early as the Paleocene epoch (65 million years ago), and archeological evidence confirms its presence in North America by the late Paleocene (55 million years ago), most probably carried across the Beringia land bridge that anciently united Alaska and Siberia. "Cornelian cherry," also known historically as "Cornel cherry," derives from the resemblance of this food plant's lustrous fruit to both the semiprecious stone "carnelian" and the true "cherry" (*Prunus cerasus*). Theophrastus labeled the Cornelian cherry fruit *kranion*, Greek for "skull," because of its intriguing shape, and, figuring largely in both Greek and Roman myth, the Cornelian cherry not only sprouted from that legendary Romulan spear, but was also traditionally believed to be the wood from which the Trojan Horse so instrumental to the sack of Troy by Odysseus was manufactured.

Although the English herbalist John Gerard did note in 1597 that "there be sundry trees of the cornel in the gardens of such as love rare and dainty plants," and, today, the Cornelian cherry is primarily grown as a decorative landscape plant, it was almost exclusively prized in antique times for its culinary and medicinal applications. Columella, in his *De Re Rustica*, instructs in the first century A.D. that "Cornel-berries . . . should be picked while they are still hard and not very ripe . . ." and, in 1629, British apothecary John Parkinson wrote that "Cornels . . . by reason of the pleasantness in them . . . are also preferred and eaten, both for rarity and delight . . ." Medicinally, the fruits of the *Cornus mas* were

CORNELIAN CHERRY

extolled for their astringent properties and, together with the bark and blossoms, as a treatment for bowel complaints, cholera, and fever. We know now that Cornelian cherries contain twice the vitamin C per weight as an orange, and, like all red fruits, contain healthy doses of cancer-fighting anthocyanins. Cornelian cherry fruit can actually be pear- ("skull"), barrel-, or oval-shaped and, depending on the cultivar, ivory colored, yellow, bright red, or deep purple when fully ripe. Like the true cherry, each fruit contains a single, large, hard seed, and flavor will vary by cultivar from the somewhat astringent to the very sweet indeed.

Fruiting is preceded in very early spring by a glorious haze of tiny sulfur-colored blossoms borne on elegant bare branches, followed by a handsome leafing out for summer, and then a copious, glossy fruiting in late summer and fall. And the final accolade we can award to the Cornelian cherry is a marvelously carefree habit, being self-fertile (although a pollinator will be appreciated for optimal productivity), adaptable to a wide range of soils and growing conditions, and performing superbly in USDA zones 4 through 8. There are many lovely varieties from which to choose; however, here let me recommend two types with the added appeal of variegated foliage: 'Aureo-elegantissima,' with green leaves outlined in yellow, and 'Variegata,' with leaves irregularly marginated in creamy white. Many gastronomes suggest that the best Cornelian cherries have a somewhat plumlike flavor and, despite Columella's recommendation, to insure optimal sweetness, most also deem it advisable to leave the fruit to ripen on the tree for as long as possible before harvesting. I suggest the concoction of a Cornelian cherry syrup for multiple excellent culinary applications: steam whole berries with a scant bit of water in a nonreactive pot until soft (about 20 minutes), mash and strain, return the liquid to the pot, add a like amount of sugar, reheat stirring until dissolved, and bottle.

🎋 15. Crabapple 'Prairie Fire' 🎋
Malus 'Prairie Fire'

"If, on being cultivated, it does not yield new and palatable varieties,
it will at least be celebrated for the beauty of its flowers,
and for the sweetness of its perfume."

—Francois-Andre Michaux, *North American Sylva*, 1819

Henry David Thoreau said in his *Wild Apples* of 1852 that, generally, crabapples were "sour enough to set a squirrel's teeth on edge and make a jay scream," and, due to this perhaps overly tart personality, crabapples have always been treated as the poor cousins of the *Malus* family. However, for spectacularly decorative habit coupled with excellent jelly-making opportunity, there's absolutely nothing to equal it. The *Pyrus malus* ("Bad Pear"), original to the Caucasus Mountains and eastern Turkey and the wild ancestor of all cultivated crabapples, was named such by Karl Linnaeus, the "Bad" (*Malus*) moniker, of course, stemming from that unfortunate incident in the Garden of Eden. The Viking invaders of eighth-century England imported, along with their marauding zeal, the word *scrabba* or *scrab* to identify the *Pyrus malus*, this later being transmuted to "crab." The popularity of the crabapple probably reached its zenith in the Middle Ages when, due to a universal lack of clean drinking water, apple cider was the pan-global beverage of choice, and was especially admired when left to "harden."

There has always been some swirling debate about what distinguishes a crabapple from a regular apple, this being finally settled in 1943 when Donald Wyman of Harvard's Arnold Arboretum pronounced in his *Crabapples in America* that "the crab apple is any member of the genus *Malus* which has fruits two inches or less in diameter." In 1984, the National Crabapple Evaluation Program, in order to evaluate and select the hardiest, best-quality, and most disease-resistant varieties available, distributed 49 crabapple cultivars to a total of 25 different United States

CRABAPPLE 'PRAIRIE FIRE'

locations. During the same period, the noted crabapple expert Father John Fiala finished compiling his definitive *Flowering Crabapples: The Genus Malus*. In both of these studies, the red-flowering crabapple 'Prairie Fire' won top laurels, Father Fiala rating 'Prairie Fire' as both "Excellent" and "Recommended," a nearly unique dual accolade. Introduced by Dr. Daniel Dayton of the University of Illinois at Urbana in 1982, this simply stunning crabapple will grow to 15 to 20 feet with a shapely rounded habit and deep red bark, making 'Prairie Fire' a decorative triumph even in the gloomiest months of winter. In May, copious crimson buds open to spectacular, large, deep pinky-red blossoms, further enhanced with deep purple/red leaves maturing to a dark bronzy green. As fall approaches the foliage transmutes to a gorgeously gregarious orange: the perfect visual foil for the shiny, 1/2-inch bright crimson fruit. Additionally, 'Prairie Fire' is extremely resistant to cedar/apple rust, fireblight, mildew, and apple scab, and is hardy to USDA zones 4 through 8. For all these sterling qualities, 'Prairie Fire' was named "Tree of the Year" in Kansas in 2002 and in Iowa in 2006. Although tolerant of a fairly wide range of soil conditions, 'Prairie Fire' will appreciate full sun, some young pruning to develop good branch structure, and good drainage and air circulation, as excessive moisture and wet soils can promote potential diseases. The astringent "verjuice" of the crabapple, rich in tannins, was widely employed historically to treat chronic diarrhea, as an anti-inflammatory and antiseptic, and a poultice made from the boiled or roasted fruit was broadly used to help heal wounds and burns and soothe sore or inflamed eyes. Although culinary verjuice is most commonly rendered from green grapes, crabapple verjuice, akin to cider vinegar, has been an age-old gastronomic staple in Europe, and is especially excellent as a flavoring for pork dishes. To prepare, simply gather ripe crabapples, mash or food process, transfer to a bowl, add water to cover, leave to ferment for 3 or 4 days, strain, forcing the juice from the pulp, and bottle.

16. Cranberry 'HyRed'
Vaccinium macrocarpon

"It has been an unchallengeable American doctrine that cranberry sauce, a pink goo with overtones of sugared tomatoes, is a delectable necessity of the Thanksgiving board and that turkey is uneatable without it."

—Alistair Cooke (1908–2004)

The "American" cranberry (*Vaccinium macrocarpon*) is native only to North America, but, being the largest-fruited of all cranberry varieties, has been naturalized to many parts of the globe. Known by a host of Native American names, it was the earliest European settlers who coined the term "crane berry," as it was thought the cranberry's small pink blossom resembled the head and bill of a crane. Native Americans employed the cranberry in myriad valuable ways, including as a natural carmine dye, mashed into a poultice to draw poison from arrow wounds, and, famously, pounded into venison to create their long-keeping, dried pemmican, the cranberry's natural benzoic acid content preserving the meat almost indefinitely. The Delaware Indians of New Jersey, who called it *pakmintzen,* were so fond of the cranberry that they revered it as an earthly symbol of peace and plenty and, of course, the Pilgrims were legendarily served cranberries by the hospitable Wampanoags at their first Thanksgiving meal in 1621. As well, because of their impressive vitamin C content and storability, barrels of cranberries could be found onboard fairly every eighteenth-century American sailing vessel as an extremely effective preventative against scurvy.

The American cultivated cranberry industry saw its birth in 1816 in Dennis, Massachusetts, when Captain Henry Hall noticed that the sand blowing in from the beaches onto his bogs improved his wild cranberry production dramatically. Hall subsequently began transplanting wild cranberry vines into manageable beds, and then topping them off with

CRANBERRY 'HYRED'

sand, a technique that soon gained mass popularity. Oddly, for a useful food plant, the cranberry is still surprisingly untamed, most modern varieties having been delivered directly from the wild. However (drum roll, please), in 1994, in a sensational bit of cranberry news, Eric Zeldin and Brent McCown of the University of Wisconsin succeeded in hybridizing the first new publicly available cranberry in more than three decades. Not only ripening a full two weeks earlier than its parent 'Stevens,' the thrilling 'HyRed' cranberry also produces berries containing three times the anthocyanin as its antecedent, making every berry an antioxidant powerhouse. As well, like all cranberries, the 'HyRed' is blissfully high in vitamin C, relatively low in calories, and a good source of fiber and potassium. And so, after some years of commercial testing in Wisconsin, Massachusetts, New Jersey, Oregon, and British Columbia, and with appropriate fanfare, the fabulous 'HyRed,' the very first cranberry to ever be awarded a patent, may now be licensed from the Wisconsin Alumni Research Foundation (WARF).

I would hazard to guess that most of you are unaware of the ornamental value of the 'HyRed' or an other cranberry as an extremely appealing low-growing ground cover. Hardy to zone 2 south to Virginia and west to Indiana and Michigan, the American cranberry, in general, boasts small, handsome, evergreen leaves that, when planted at 1-foot intervals, will grow into a solid, 10-inch-high thatch of pleasing deep greenery. Additionally, their pretty white-to-pink flowers will bloom in June and July, followed by the familiar supremely decorative red fruit in fall. Contrary to popular misconception, cranberries do not need or even care for "bogs." What they prefer is an acid peat soil with a top dressing of sand (although they will grow perfectly well in ordinary garden soil), plenty of sun, and regular watering. With proper care, cranberries can produce for 100 years or more, and one 5-foot-square patch will reward you with up to 5 pounds a year of fruit once established. Despite Alistair Cooke's uncharitable pronouncement, why not make the simplest of cranberry sauces by boiling 2 parts cranberries to 1 part each water and refined sugar until suitably thickened?

❦ 17. Currant 'Pink Champagne' ❦
18. Currant 'Titania'
Ribes vulgare, Ribes nigrum

Scottish lore held that good fortune would surely follow if, after the wedding ceremony, in an apparently ancient show of "tough love," the mother of the bride met her at the door and broke a currant bun over her head.

Confusion has hounded this berry-bearing family historically, as the true currant (*Ribes* spp.) became incorrectly commingled with the far more ancient Zante grape (*Vitis vinifera*), generally exported from the Greek city of Corinth and known continentally as *Raisin de Corauntz,* because of their physical similarity when dried. *Corauntz* somehow managed to attach itself to the grape's dried *Ribes* double and, however erroneous, the name stuck. *Ribes,* native to the northern hemispheres of most continents, count the European red, pink, and white currants (*R. rubrum, R. petraeum, R. sativum*, and *R. vulgare*) and the European and Asian black currants (*R. nigrum and R. ussuriense*) among its constituents. The German-Swiss naturalist Conrad Gesner was known to have selected a variety of *Ribes petraeum* to transplant into his garden in 1561, and the British herbalist William Turner said of the red currant in 1568: "Ribes is a little bushe . . . and in the tops . . . are red berries in clusters in taste at the first something sower but pleasant enough when they are fully ripe." In the seventeenth century, however, John Gerard noted the black currant's "stinking and somewhat loathing savour," clearly in reference to this type's famously unaromatic foliage, thought by nondevotees to be regrettably redolent of cat pee.

Writing about the current state of currant culture in the United States has been entirely vexatious to me: while European currants, introduced into America with the earliest English settlers, enjoyed considerable popularity for both their medicinal and culinary merits for hundreds of years, the horticultural tide turned against them at the turn of the twentieth

Currant 'Pink Champagne'

century, and they were unjustly accused of spreading white pine blister rust (*Cronartium ribicola*), a disease lethal to 5-needle pine trees. By 1912, in order to protect the more lucrative lumber industry, both federal and state restrictions had been placed on the import and culture of *Ribes* species, black currants in particular being targeted as the most pernicious hosts of the disease. By 1920, not only had an all-out federal ban been placed on black currants, but various northern states had also passed embargos on essentially all *Ribes* cultivars, and a national program of eradication or severe limitation was promptly implemented. As one might expect, this pretty much queered the currant market in America.

Eventually, however, it was discovered that, rather than *spreading* white pine blister rust, the *Ribes* family were, in fact, as much victims as their arboreal neighbors, although the fact that they served as "hosts" for the disease still made them unpopular in those areas in which culture of 5-needle pines was important. So, while the federal statute was rescinded in 1966, to this day restrictive laws regarding *Ribes* import and culture (again, primarily in regard to the black types) remain on the books in Delaware, Maine, Massachusetts, Michigan, New Hampshire, New Jersey, North Carolina, Ohio, Rhode Island, Virginia, and West Virginia. Here, however, let us also bear in mind that the black currant is by far the favored darling of gastronomic Europe (think *Cassis* and the wonderful French jam confection *Bar Le Duc*), and that black currants alone offer twice the antioxidancy of blueberries, four times the vitamin C of oranges, and twice the potassium of bananas. Therefore, my thorny dilemma is this: should I recommend a black currant variety to you, or not?

And, just to add another dash of contrariness to this agricultural maelstrom, even before the white pine panic, although esteemed on the continent, in the United States, black currants ran a distant fourth in popularity behind the red, white, and pink varieties, in part because of the unpleasant scent of their foliage and also because their exceptionally tart taste makes them almost wholly unsuitable for fresh consumption. As John Hedrick, author of the classic *Small Fruits of New York,* commented in 1925: "Few Americans born in the country have tasted the fruit or, ever having done so, care for a second taste." After much agitation, my decision has been to, indeed, recommend one modern, nicely rust-resistant, and very healthful black currant hybrid, knowing full well that some will be unable to grow it, and one gorgeous pink heirloom variety, which will hopefully be available to most of you.

Although not the easiest of food crops, to my mind, currants, particularly, the red, white, and pink varieties, are the "crown jewels" of the fruit world, their glistening, implausibly translucent bunches of fruit looking for all the world like clusters of ruby, crystal, and tourmaline beads when illuminated by the sun. And one of the most marvelous of these edible dazzlers must surely be the antique European variety 'Pink Champagne' (*Ribes vulgare*), which name goes a good way in describing the unique allure of these berries. 'Pink Champagne' is a handsome bush, growing from 3 to 5 feet with a vigorous, upright habit and a deciduous cladding of attractive 3-lobed blue/green leaves. However, it is the tasty, sweet/tart fruit that is its primary glory, being a beautifully rich, clear, "champagne" pink. As well, these gorgeous, gemlike clusters are preceded by smallish green flowers running the length of 5- or 6-inch stems, known as a "strigs," giving the bush a lovely, lacy quality in spring.

The black currant I will commend to you here is the 1984 Swedish introduction 'Titania,' and I recommend this Nordic belle to you, firstly, because, true to her name, she is a queen of heartiness and strength, and, secondly and perhaps most importantly, she is totally immune to the dreaded white pine blister rust as well as having a good resistance to powdery mildew. Additionally, her fruit size is large, her posture extremely vigorous (reaching heights to 6 feet), she will gain her full maturity in three seasons versus the four or five common to most other varieties, and she's adapted to USDA zones 3 through 8.

Currants are native to cooler climes and will sulk and swoon in extended high temperatures and humidity, and their leaves are prone to scorching in direct sun, so both of these varieties will enjoy part shade and a good layer of mulch to keep their feet cool. Also, a good fall pruning to selected second- and third-year canes will not go unrewarded. As all currants contain a number of tiny seeds (in antique times tediously removed with a quill before consumption), the best place to start for a fresh currant recipe is with strained juice: clean 2 pounds of currants, remove stems, and steam for an hour to extract about 5 cups. For 'Titania,' reboil with a

CURRANT 'TITANIA'

cup of sugar and a quarter cup lemon juice, mix 1 part juice with 3 parts water or seltzer, and serve this refreshing beverage over ice. For 'Pink Champagne' why not reboil with 2 cups of sugar till nicely thickened, cool, and serve as a delicate pink sauce perfect for meats and desserts?

🎋 19. Date Palm 🎋
Phoenix spp.

"Shake the trunk of the palm tree towards thee:
it will drop fresh, ripe dates upon thee.
Eat, then, and drink, and let thine eye be gladdened!"

—Koran 19:25–26

Originally native to the Persian Gulf, date palms have sustained and sheltered humankind, particularly of the desert, since before human memory, and have been revered as symbols of both peace and victory ever since man came, quite literally, to his senses. The Koran reports that, when the Virgin Mary was pregnant with the Savior (or "prophet" in Islam), she was sent the heavenly directive italicized above. The great early-nineteenth-century French botanist Augustin Pyramus de Candolle claimed that, in our prehistory, date palms forested the area from Senegal to India's Indus Valley, and archeological evidence confirms that wild date palms were growing in Iran, Egypt, and Pakistan by 5000 B.C. On January 25, 2005, Dr. Elaine Solowey of the Arava Institute for Environmental Studies planted a date palm (*Phoenix dactylifera*) seed unearthed from the ancient site of Herod's palace atop Mount Masada in Israel. Five weeks later, the seed, carbon dated from 65 to 35 B.C., sprouted, eventually into a tree now known universally as the "Methuselah Palm." As of February 6, 2006, this infant yet ancient fruit plant had 5 fine-looking fronds.

Date palms are, of course, sacred to Christian religions, their fronds being symbolically woven into crosses on Palm Sunday, and Psalms 92:12–14 rhapsodizing: "The righteous will flourish like a palm tree . . ." Dates were most probably carried into the Roman Empire with the legions of the Emperor Vespasian sometime after 73 A.D., and they were delivered into North America via California by Franciscan and Jesuit missionaries in 1765. However, unfortunately, this does not mean that you

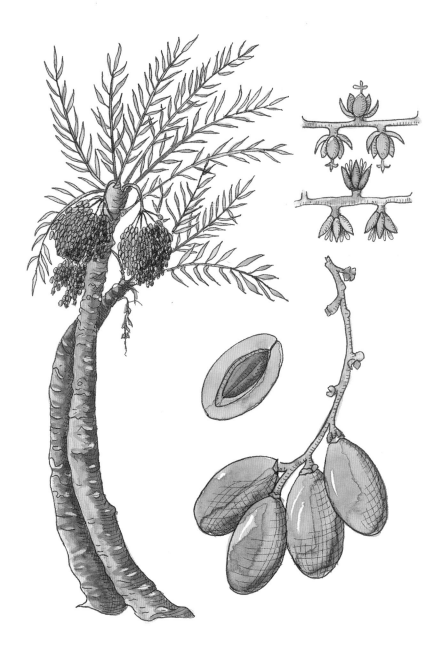

DATE PALM

can have one—or, at least, one that will bear edible fruit, as date palms crave hot, dry conditions, California and Arizona being our only two states with any significant edible date production. However, if you are in USDA zones 10 or 11, an edible date palm could well be in your future, and a handsome future it will be: some varieties grow to 120 feet with leaves up to 20 feet long, and most bear for 100 years or more. Psalms 92:14 goes on to say of "the righteous," in clear reference to the date palm: "They will still bear fruit in old age, they will stay fresh and green."

Phoenix roebelenii, the southeast Asian Pygmy date, is the variety I will recommend to the greatest number of you here (those in zones 10 and 11 may try the *Phoenix dactylifera 'Khadrawy'*), as it is a magnificent plant for pot culture, although, sadly, the dates it produces are inedible. Stave your tears, however, for this is a supremely decorative landscape and "interior-scape" plant, reaching a height of 6 to 12 feet with a graceful single trunk and dense crown of 3-foot, glossy green leaves. *Phoenix* palms are dioecious, so only the female can produce, and, to do so, she will need an injection of pollen from an accommodating male, so if you want fruit, you will need some of each. Date palms, aside from their preference for nonhumid heat, have negligible nutrient requirements and are both drought- and poor-soil-tolerant, and trees will start producing in 5 to 6 years from planting. Dates, which are an excellent source of vitamin C, with each date containing about 23 calories, ripen in 4 stages: *kimri* (unripe), *khalal* (full-size, crunchy), *rutab* (ripe, soft), and *tamr* (ripe, sun-dried). Mature females produce "bunches" of them, as many as 10, and a single large bunch can contain up to 1,000 fruits, so, if you plant an edible sort, get ready. My advice? Grow a grove of potted pygmies poolside and get your ration of the ancient and esteemed date at your local store.

20. Dewberry
21. Loganberry
22. Boysenberry
❧ 23. Tayberry ❧
Rubus hybrids

Oddly, it was the discovery of the boysenberry that gave rise to America's very first theme park, Knott's Berry Farm in Buena Park, California, currently the twelfth most-visited amusement park in America.

Making the acquaintance of the *Rubus* family is exactly like stepping into an enormous bramble patch: endlessly and painfully dense and thorny. As we have discussed, there is a colossal brood of nearly indistinguishable progeny in this global clan and, therefore, in this chapter, I have chosen to offer up not one but four closely related blackberry hybrids: the dewberry, the loganberry, the boysenberry, and the tayberry. Although there are seemingly infinite varieties similar to these that are still referred to as blackberries, these four, along with others we will wrestle to the ground in a later chapter, happened to have been selected and alternately named, mainly by and for their developers. To my mind, however, they are all actually dewberries with identity crises and the dewberry alone is a legitimate blackberry subset, for unlike most, which grow on erect caning bushes, dewberries (*Rubus pubescens*) are creepy-crawly things that spread along the ground, forming a dense, prickly mat.

All of these share the attributes of the dewberry crawling habit, white, 5-petaled flowers, prickly stems, signature *Rubus* leaves, and fruit that looks approximately like a blackberry, although they can vary from sweet to somewhat bitter, black to reddish, and, on the bush, from nicely abundant to tiresomely scarce. For instance, unhybridized dewberries, i.e., those that have remained genetically unaltered from the wild, seem

DEWBERRY

LOGANBERRY

to generally deliver sweet but sparse fruit, sometimes only several to a plant. However, in true, contrary *Rubus* fashion, the Swamp dewberry (*Rubus hispidus*) is a bramble native to eastern North America, but the berries are thought to be too bitter for culinary use.

Although the loganberry has gone out of style culinarily, at one time it was potentially the most important berry crop ever grown in Oregon's berry-rich Willamette Valley. Developed in 1880 by home gardener Judge John H. Logan of Santa Cruz, California, by crossing an 'Antwerp' red raspberry with two blackberry varieties, one the 'Aughinbaugh,' the result was a tart red berry too acidic for fresh consumption but excellent when sweetened for cordials and pies. Although it did not travel well and was ultimately pretty much abandoned as a food crop, it was wildly popular between about 1920 and 1930, and its unique provenance created broad interest in using it as a breeder.

Just to confuse matters a little more thoroughly, most botanists feel that the boysenberry is a hybrid developed by crossing a blackberry with both a raspberry and a loganberry, and the tayberry is a cross between a loganberry and a black raspberry. Distinguished from other dewberry/blackberry descendants by its reddish-purple fruit and dust-like coating, the boysenberry is notable for its development as well, which was nearly lost. In 1928, George Darrow of the USDA and local berry grower Walter Knott went in search of a large, flavorful, reddish-purple berry being developed by Anaheim California Parks superintendent Rudolf Boysen. They learned that Boysen had abandoned his hybridizing and sold his farm; however, the persevering Darrow and Knott managed to locate several frail, surviving vines on the former Boysen acreage, and transplanted them to Knott's farm in Buena Park. Knott finally began selling the boysenberry and his wife's homemade boysenberry jam in 1935, this mom-and-pop enterprise ultimately growing to become the Knott's Berry Farm theme park. The tayberry, which was released in 1979 by the Scottish Horticultural Research Institute and named after the River Tay, is thought by many to be the tastiest of this confusing family, bearing plentiful crops of sweetly tart, cone-shaped, deep red/purple berries up to an inch and a half long.

Like most *Rubus* family members, all of these four are happily high

BOYSENBERRY

TAYBERRY

in vitamin C, fiber, and anthocyanins but, culturally, these cultivars are, of course, defiantly different. For instance, while dewberries and tayberries seem to be tough as iron, boysenberries prefer a mild climate, although they can be grown in colder regions if mulched sufficiently in winter. As well, one of the historic problems with loganberries and, currently, with boysenberries, is that they are quite soft constitutionally, which makes them nearly impossible to ship: if I were to choose one of these prickly siblings for home culture, I think I'd try the tayberry. All four may be propagated from root cuttings and are most easily grown (and picked) when trained up trellises or wire frames, and, like all *Rubus* descendants, new stems will sprout yearly, but only the second-year *floracanes* will bear fruit. As all of these berries are on the tart side, a cobbler would be an excellent employment. Therefore, toss the berries with sugar, a dash of both cornstarch and lemon juice, cook till thickened, and then pour into a baking dish and top with a mixture of a cup each of flour and sugar, 2 teaspoons of baking powder, a moistening of milk, a pinch of salt, an egg, and a knob of butter. Bake for about half an hour at 350 degrees, cool, and serve triumphantly with vanilla ice cream.

24. Russian Olive
25. Autumn Olive
❦ 26. Goumi ❦
Elaeagnus angustifolia, Elaeagnus umbellata,
Elaeagnus multiflora

In ancient Persia, the fragrant blossoms of the Elaeagnus *were thought to have such a libidinal effect on women that, when the trees were in bloom, men habitually kept their wives and daughters under lock and key.*

The *Elaeagnus* family is a genus comprised of somewhere between 50 and 70 highly decorative and scented flowering plants mostly native to the temperate and subtropical regions of Eurasia. However, only 3 of these siblings, the Russian olive, *E. angustifolia*, the Autumn olive, *E. umbellata*, and the Goumi (or "gumi"), *E. multiflora*, are blessed with edible fruit, and they are the ones that will pique our interest here. Despite the fact that, except in the look of their silvery leaves, the *Elaeagnus* family is totally unrelated to the "true" olive family (*Olea europaea*), the botanical name *Elaeagnus* derives from *elaia*, the Greek word for olive oil, which, in turn, finds its roots in "Elais." One of the three granddaughters of Dionysos, Elais, along with her sisters Oeno and Spermo, were the goddesses of oil, wine, and grain respectively, each having the power to turn whatever she touched into her proprietary foodstuff, which must have been extremely satisfying on one level and extremely trying on another. The *agnus* component derives from the Greek *hagnos*, meaning "pure," therefore, *Elaeagnus* adding up to "pure olive oil," which as we have noted, it is not.

There are many American botanists whose mouths will gape and eyes spark at the mere notion that I have chosen to list the *Elaeagnus* family in this tome. Honestly, they are not without their reasons; for one, both Russian and Autumn olives are currently on invasive plant lists in many

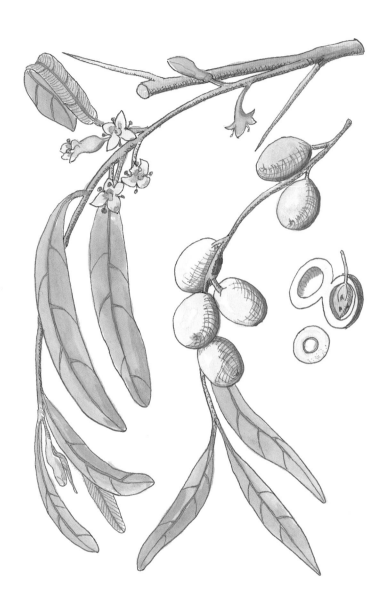

RUSSIAN OLIVE

Autumn Olive

GOUMI

to most of our united states. However, with both of these, it was a clear and tragic case of young love gone awry, as they were happily imported into the United States from Asia in 1830 with the greatest fanfare and goodwill. For, aside from their physical beauty, their drought resistance and almost unique ability to fix nitrogen in the soil through their tenacious root systems allowed them to not only thrive even in the poorest soils, but to enrich and "hold" them as well, and they were used extensively upon their import to reforest severely eroded and reclaimed land. Additionally, as both Russian and Autumn olives grow rapidly and will begin to fruit in as early as 3 years, they made a brilliant and nearly instant wildlife cover and food source.

The only catch was that they proved a mite *too* hardy. Seed spread by birds and other wildlife soon started sprouting everywhere, particularly in vacant grass and pasture lands, roadside ditches, and so on, and these are plants that respond to both cutting and burning with an even stronger growth habit. As late as 1975 both Russian and Autumn olives were described as "rarely escaping from cultivation," but currently, the Russian olive is virtually naturalized and viewed as potentially problematic in 36 of our 50 states, and the Autumn olive in 27. Therefore, a good many of you probably have a Russian or Autumn olive growing somewhere not 10 feet from you. And, while the goumi (also known as the 'Cherry Elaeagnus') is far less prevalent and far more benign in terms of invasive qualities, it would be wise to check with your local authorities before planting any one of these. However, should you find one in your environs, do go investigate.

First of all, this is a lovely family indeed, with both the Russian and Autumn olives growing to about 20 feet with a virtually identical graceful, somewhat shrubby habit, olivelike foliage, tiny but intensely fragrant yellow flowers, and distinctive silvery "scales" dappling the young stems, leaves, flowers, and fruit. Their distinguishing characteristics are that the Autumn olive has somewhat rounder and greener leaves and deep red, dime-sized, round fruit, while the Russian olive boasts slimmer, more lanceolate, grayer leaves and yellow to orange berries. The goumi, on the other hand, is a true shrub, typically growing to 6 to 8 feet with green, silver-bellied ovate leaves and silver-dappled golden fruit ripening to red. And, as you might guess, all are mightily adaptable to anything but deep, wet shade and are hardy to USDA zones 3 (Russian olive), 4 (Autumn olive), and 5 (goumi).

However, what really sets this pretty if somewhat overly zealous plant family apart is the incredible health potential of their fruit, as all 3 are chockablock with vitamins (A, C, and E) and antioxidants, with each berry containing as much as 10 times the lycopene per weight as a tomato. Fruit taste can be somewhat variable, with the goumi habitually winning the tastiest accolades, and, in general, fruit should be picked when very ripe, as even slightly under-ripe fruit can be mouth-puckeringly astringent. The flavor of a good, ripe *Elaeagnus* berry is said to be reminiscent of both currants and cranberries, so my advice is to go pick some from your neighborhood wild (or plant a goumi and wait a few years) and whip up a sprightly *Elaeagnus* sauce (another simmer, sieve, and conquer idea) to accompany a roast fowl: simmer 4 cups of *Elaeagnus* berries in 1/4 cup water until soft, mash and sieve, add 1/3 cup sugar, bring to a boil, reduce heat, cover, and cook until thickened (about 10 minutes).

❧ 27. Elderberry 'Black Beauty' ❧
Sambucus nigra

"For hours beneath the elder-tree
She broods beside the stream;
Her dark eyes filled with mystery,
Her dark soul rapt in dream."

—William Sharp, "The Death-Child" (1837–1895)

Elderberry is a shrub so ornamental that I, personally, am always amazed that it also bears such deliciously prolific and decorative fruit. A member of the honeysuckle family, *Caprifoliaceae* (signifying "goat leaves" as its leaves are believed to be shaped like the ear of a goat), the elderberry's botanical name *Sambucus* comes to us from the Greek *sambuke*, an ancient stringed instrument traditionally fashioned from elder wood. The common name "elder" derives from the Anglo-Saxon *aeld*, meaning "fire," and Stone Age evidence indicates that, as long as 10,000 years ago, elder wood was used as primitive tinder and the hollowed stems as blow tubes to coax embers into flame. This incendiary heritage seems to have given birth to a true dichotomy of associations in many civilizations for the elder not only embodied the sacred and the spiritual, but the opposing elements of necromancy and black witchcraft as well. So in some cultures, an elder cross might be nailed to a barn to protect the herd inside, while, at the same moment, countless weepy poems (like the one above) insisted on placing forlorn ghosts in the gloomy shade of spectral elder trees. This darker reference clearly stems from the popular medieval belief that the biblical traitor Judas hanged himself from an elder tree.

On the other hand, the English writer Lady Rosalind Northcote, in her *Book of Herbs* of 1903, states: "The Russians believe that Elder-trees drive away evil spirits, and the Bohemians go to it with a spell to take away fever. The Sicilians think that sticks of its wood will . . . drive away

ELDERBERRY 'BLACK BEAUTY'

robbers, and the Serbs introduce a stick of Elder into their wedding ceremonies to bring good luck." In Celtic lore, *Eld* was the land of the fairies, and it was believed that if one sat beneath an elder tree on Midsummer's Eve, one would see the miracle of the Fairy King passing. Elder also constituted an antique herbal remedy of significant note, being known throughout much of early history as "the medicine chest of the common man." For instance, in parts of medieval Europe, it was believed that elder could cure rheumatism, a belief manifested by lashing elder twig hoops to the body parts in question, and, in other cultures, it was believed that water taken from a malade's bath and sprinkled on the roots of an elder tree would transmit the illness to the accommodating plant. Modern herbalists use the flowers and fruits of the elder for infusions for such diverse maladies as fever, headache, cold, rheumatism, and consumption.

There are many beautiful varieties of elder, all offering frothy white to pink blossoms and leaf colorations running from regulation green to yellow and purple, with a good number of interesting variegations and pretty marginations in between. 'Black Beauty,' introduced from England in 2002, is the reigning purple-leafed darling, boasting extremely ornamental black/purple foliage, its leaves actually becoming darker as the season progresses. Tiny flowers form huge, deep pink, headily lemon-scented blossoms, followed by clusters of glossy, dramatically dark purple berries in late summer. 'Black Beauty,' being hardy to USDA zone 4, is, like most elders, a wonderfully adaptive and uncomplaining shrub, although like certain other elderberries, will also require a second cultivar as companion in order to set the best fruit. The concoction of some tasty elderflower cordial of a summer weekend would be an excellent exercise for this dusky garden stunner. Pour 6 pints of boiling water over 2 pounds of sugar, stir till dissolved, and then, when cooled, add 2 sliced oranges, 3 sliced lemons, a packet of citric acid, and 30 elderflower heads. Let steep in a cool place for a day, and then strain into a bottle and enjoy on a sultry summer evening.

28. Fig 'Hardy Chicago'
29. Fig 'Petite Negra'
Ficus carica

In 528 B.C., Siddhartha Gautama attained true enlightenment and founded Buddhism while sitting under a fig tree.

As every art historian knows, remove a fig leaf and uncover something sensational. Botanically, the edible fig may constitute the most remarkable form of fruit on earth, as it is not actually a fruit at all, but a hollow receptacle entirely lined with tiny flowers, which, in total darkness, manage to bloom and ripen seeds: that ruby or emerald flesh of which so many cultures have been so fond is actually a miniature (and nearly divine) interior carpet of spent blossoms! Both the Assyrians and ancient Sumerians adored the fig as long ago as 2900 B.C., and figs were known in Crete by 1600 B.C., the early Greeks prizing them so highly that, in the original Olympic Games, it was a fig leaf wreath rather than a laurel that crowned the victors. In 717 B.C., Romulus and Remus, the fraternal founders of Rome, were said to be suckled by a she-wolf in the shade of an accommodating fig tree.

Figs also figured prominently in the *Odyssey*, as Homer narrates the agonies of Tantulus in the underworld: "Trees spread their foliage high over the pool and dangle fruits above his head . . . sweet figs and luxuriant olives," as well as in the Bible, as in this passage from Numbers 20:5 concerning the flight of the children of Israel: "And why have you made us come up out of Egypt to bring us to this evil place? It is no place for grain or figs . . ." Fig poultices also rated a mention in the Bible, Isaiah 38:21 reporting: "Let them take a lump of figs, and lay it for a plaister upon the boil, and he shall recover," and it is also known that Xerxes, king of Persia from 485 to 465 B.C., consumed Attic figs in quantity as a daily reminder of the wisdom of conquering a country that could produce something so exquisite.

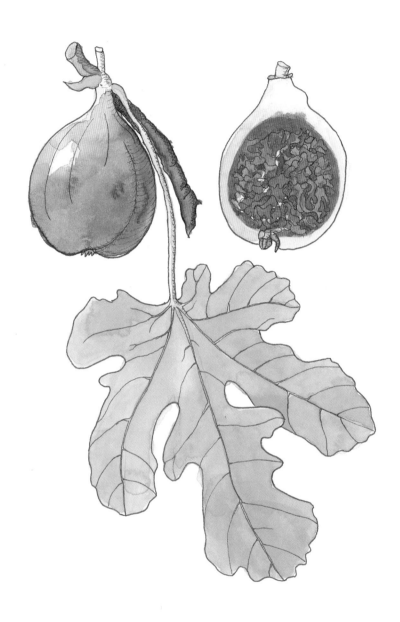

FIG 'HARDY CHICAGO'

Fig 'Petite Negra'

Mithridates, Greek king of Pontus (120–63 B.C.), who regularly consumed sublethal doses of the most popular poisons so that he might never succumb to them, proclaimed the fig to be a great and general panacea, and Greek athletes were fed almost entirely on figs, as it was believed they increased both strength and swiftness. Pliny the Elder reports in the first century A.D. that figs formed a large portion of the food of slaves, especially agricultural workers, noting no less than 29 different varieties under cultivation in Greece, and further reported: "Figs are . . . the best food that can be eaten by those who are brought low by long sickness . . . They increase the strength of young people, preserve the elderly in better health and make them look younger with fewer wrinkles." Additionally, in Dionysian revels, fig is the wood of choice for phallic worshippers.

Spanish and Portuguese missionaries imported figs into the Americas in the early sixteenth century, fig shipments being recorded from Seville to the West Indies in 1520. By 1526, fig trees were growing in what is now contemporary Cuba and had been introduced into Peru by 1528—the oldest living fig tree in the New World, the Pizarro Tree, planted in 1538, still stands at the governor's palace in Lima. From Cuba, figs reached the coast of the Carolinas by 1575, were introduced into Florida by 1579, into Virginia via Bermuda in 1621, and into the Louisiana Territory by French missionaries in 1720. In about 1769, the fig made its way into California with Franciscan and Jesuit missionaries, who, as they founded increasingly northerly missions, eventually planted fig trees from San Diego to Sonoma, giving California's famous "Mission fig" its ultimate sobriquet.

As you might have guessed, figs are, for the most part, temperate-to-subtropical plants, choosing to thrive best in hot, arid, "Mediterranean" conditions but, with the correct protection in winter, they can also prosper as far north as USDA zone 6b. Therefore, here I have chosen to offer up to you two of the most hardy types, one of which is entirely appropriate to pot culture for those of you in our most northerly zones. As owning your own fig tree is the gustatory equivalent of having a Whistler over your mantel and a Daimler in your garage, I really urge each of you to give one of these a try.

'Hardy Chicago,' the optimistically named newcomer on the fig horizon, is supposedly hardier than either of the reigning favorites 'Brown Turkey' and 'Celeste,' although many believe that one or potentially both of them must certainly play a part in the parentage of 'Hardy Chicago.' Alternately, 'Hardy Chicago' is claimed to be an import from Mount Etna in Sicily, or a product of grower Fred Born's efforts in Crystal River, Florida, with a seedling purchased from an Italian grower in Chicago. As you can see, there remains some debate concerning this contemporary creature from the mists. All that said, what isn't debatable is that 'Hardy Chicago' is *at least* as hardy as 'Celeste' and 'Brown Turkey,' its purple-blushed fruit and luscious strawberry-colored flesh are much prized for their impressively sweet, rich savor, and some even claim 'Hardy Chicago' will fruit on new suckers in spring even if it dies back entirely in winter.

However, for our indisputably cooler precincts, where your fig will have to be brought indoors in winter for successful cultivation, here we will pause to laud the merits of the modern dwarf hybrid fig 'Petite Negra,' also known as the 'Black Jack' fig. Growing to just 6 to 8 feet tall and 3 to 4 feet wide, the happily self-fertile 'Petite Negra' is diminutive enough for pot culture, yet lovely enough, with its graceful branching and dark green, lobed foliage, to be an agreeable specimen tree in your yard. And, although the first year will probably yield just a single crop, from then on, your 'Petite Negra' will offer up two annual harvests of large, sweet, deep aubergine-skinned, ruby-fleshed fruit a year.

As with all figs, a warm, sunny, southern-facing wall will increase your chances of perennial success immeasurably, and, certainly, in USDA zones 6 and below, if you are intent on keeping your 'Hardy Chicago' or 'Petite Negra' out of doors, mulching and even "burying" will be a worthwhile endeavor, "burying" entailing bending your tree to the ground, anchoring it, and topping it off with a fat layer of mulch. For less pliable models, a tarpaulin sheath stuffed with hay or leaves can also work and, for those of you in our frostiest climes, wheel your fig into a space in which the temperature will not dip below 20 degrees and water occasionally through its dormancy. Culinarily, try either of these luscious beauties split, buttered with mascarpone, wrapped in a shred of prosciutto, and then sprinkled with lemon juice and fresh ground pepper. Pure ambrosia.

30. Gooseberry 'Poorman'
Ribes grossularia

An Old English Wives' Tale holds that one may cure a sty on the eyelid by pointing a gooseberry thorn at the unsightly blemish and chanting nine times in succession: "Away, away, away!"

Here we will weigh the merits of that *Ribes* constituent the gooseberry, which many botanists believe may even be primevally ancient due to the bristly fruit of the wildest sorts, and which numbers nearly 5,000 varieties. There are, however, three basic gooseberry types: the European gooseberries (*Ribes grossularia* and *Ribes uva-crispa*), the first being bristly skinned and indigenous to northern Europe, the second being smooth-skinned and native to the Caucasus, and the American gooseberry (*Ribes hirtellum*), which is native to the north of the American continent. Due to their affinity for cooler climes, their thorny, near-weedy ubiquitousness in their native habitats, and the uneven savor of their fruit, gooseberries achieved literally no botanical mention among the ancient Romans and Greeks. Their first mention in Europe takes place in England in 1276, when they were listed in purchases for the Westminster garden of Edward I, and it is in England almost exclusively that the fairly ignored gooseberry finally found a welcoming gastronomic home, John Gerard reporting in 1597 that "There be divers sorte . . . some greater, some lesse, some rounde, others long . . . These plants do grow in London gardens and elsewhere in great abundance."

By the mid-eighteenth century, culture of the gooseberry in home gardens in Great Britain had become so popular that gooseberry clubs were formed, with members in fierce competition for the largest, meatiest fruit, culminating in the development of the massive 'London' gooseberry, which claimed the thorny crown for 36 years running. The large, sweet, green-skinned fruit most of us identify as the edible gooseberry is one of the European types, *Ribes grossularia*, grown almost exclusively in

GOOSEBERRY 'POORMAN'

England and rampantly prone to mildew in the United States. The American gooseberry, *Ribes hirtellum*, while better acclimated to our precincts, generally produces small, dark, almost inedibly tart fruit, and both types are possessed of a prickly demeanor that is beyond daunting in terms of harvest, the English botanist John Parkinson commenting in 1629 that the plant was "armed with verie sharpe and cruell crooked thorns." Additionally, all *Ribes* berries contain from 3 to 12 tiny seeds, which makes both processing and fresh eating a trial, and, as we have discussed, many *Ribes* family members were banned entirely from culture in the United States for most of the twentieth century, and are still illegal in some states. Is anyone still with me?

If so, turn your attention to the relatively modern gooseberry hybrid 'Poorman,' which, while classified as *R. grossularia*, was bred by a Mr. Craighead in Utah in 1888 as a further mating of the early European/American hybrids 'Houghton' and 'Downing.' 'Poorman' is a hearty and reliable producer of handsome, wine-red, 1-inch berries with smooth skins and excellent flavor and aroma which, while small in comparison to the European types, are the largest of any American gooseberry. Additionally, 'Poorman' is highly resistant to white pine blister rust, gray mold, and mildew, which, due to the *Ribes* clan's susceptibility to these trying diseases, is a very happy thing indeed, as is the fact that 'Poorman' produces fewer of those "cruell crooked" thorns than most, and is adaptable to USDA zones 4 to 8. As with all *Ribes*, cool temperatures, a good mulching, adequate air circulation, and some annual pruning to the strongest second-year canes will be of the essence. And, as each 'Poorman' berry's complement of tiny seeds still makes them a culinary challenge, why not try them in a classic fifteenth-century Gooseberry Fool? Simmer 1 pound of berries, 1 ounce of butter, and 2 tablespoons of sugar over low heat until soft, mash enthusiastically, pass through a sieve, cool, fold in an equal amount of whipped cream, chill, and serve to gastronomic accolades.

31. Grape 'Concord'
32. Grape 'Neptune'
Vitis labrusca

*"And Noah began to be an husbandman, and he planted a vineyard:
And he drank of the wine, and was drunken; and he was uncovered
within his tent."*

—Genesis 9:20–21

Piths of the wild *Vitis vinifera silvestris* have been found in Stone Age settlements from Germany to Cyprus, indicating consumption by *Homo erectus* a million years ago at the very least and, in the case of the grape, it seems impossible to separate this antediluvian food plant from its fermented nectar. As far back as the sixth millennium B.C., in most every ancient reference and from myriad archeological evidence, the grape had already made its transition to wine; in 1980, a wine jug unearthed at the site of Hajji Firuz Tepe in the northern Zagros Mountains of Iran dated to the Neolithic era and a very distant 5400 to 5000 B.C. During the Archaic Period in Egypt (3050–2705 B.C.), under the first two dynasties, pharaohs were buried with vast quantities of the nectar of the grape to slake their thirst in the afterlife, and in Late Uruk Mesopotamia (3500–3100 B.C.), at least the upper classes were enjoying wine with becoming regularity.

In Greco-Roman myth, Dionysos (or Bacchus) was the Thracian god of wine, representing, among other fine things, wine's power to "liberate" one's self from restraint and self-consciousness, and it seems Dionysos had a single grand mission in life: to encourage his disciples to share a dish of wine, banish care and worry, and dance to the music of the pan flute. If this led to the dipping of a toe into the inviting waters of ecstatic and orgiastic excess, well, much as many of us felt in the 1970s— how liberating! On the other side of the traditional coin, the liquor of the grape has also played a showy role in both Jewish and Christian ceremony

Grape 'Concord'

as, in Jewish ritual, the Sabbath starts with a blessing chanted over a shared goblet of wine, and in the Christian faith, wine not only constitutes the first of Christ's miracles at Cana, but also serves an important symbolic role, along with the host, as the Eucharistic "body and blood" offered to the faithful.

Allow me take a slight grape detour here and delve into the mysteries of what is known in health circles as the "French paradox," the conundrum being this: why do the French, who consume vast quantities of red meat, preferably smothered in butter and cream, and smoke like a gaggle of teenage girls with bad attitude, also suffer a 42 percent lower incidence of heart attacks? Beginning in 1982, it was ultimately proven that the anthocyanin resveratrol, an organic compound found in red wine, was a great part of the answer, helping to inhibit the formation of cancer cells and reduce the buildup of fat in the arteries, the highest concentrations, 10 to 12 times higher than *Vitis vinifera,* being found in the muscadines. As you might expect, red wine sales, particularly in the health-conscious United States, skyrocketed, and the "French paradox" was solved to the immense satisfaction of the French, of course. You'll also be happy to know that wine drinkers have much less chance of succumbing to Alzheimer's and senile dementia than teetotalers or hard drinkers, so my advice is to get out your corkscrew.

There are three main types of grape: *Vitis vinifera,* the ancient Eurasian variety, thought to have originated near the Caspian Sea in Asia Minor, and *Vitis labrusca* and *Vitis rotundifolia,* both impressively antique American varieties, the *Vitis labrusca* variety growing with such wild early profligacy from Canada south to the Carolinas that, in the tenth century, the Viking explorers named Canada "Vinland." *Vitis rotundifolia,* the touchy yet very healthful muscadines, are original to Virginia south to central Florida and west to Texas, and are rarely grown outside their native habitat. Hardiness has also been a major limiting factor for the culture of *vinifera* grapes in the United States, making the earliest East Coast attempts at their cultivation in the New World sadly ineffective. Therefore, it is to two brilliant *labrusca* types I will turn in this chapter, although, if you live in the South, do investigate some of the tasty, particularly healthy, and disease-resistant muscadine types available.

Seedless grapes to be eaten fresh are basically an early-nineteenth-century invention, and the estimable seedless trait in table grapes is almost exclusively derived from the marriage of the antique types 'Thompson Seedless' and 'Black Monukka,' with current hybridization focusing on improved quality, skin texture, berry size, crack resistance, and adaptation to a broader range of zones. With all those factors in mind, the admirable 'Neptune' grape was released for culture by the University of Arkansas in 1998. 'Neptune' is a *Vitis labrusca* that bears a striking resemblance to its familiar 'Thompson Seedless' parent but with far greater adaptation to East Coast (read "humid" and "changeable") conditions. 'Neptune' will tempt you with handsome yellow/green fruit borne in lavish clusters with a fine, sweet, fruity flavor and, of course, that happily seedless habit. Additionally, this rambling, woody vine, swathed in handsome notched leaves, also shows good-to-excellent resistance to fruit cracking, black rot, anthracnose, and mildews.

Now, let us turn our attention to that hero of PB and J-dom, the Concord grape. First bred by Ephraim Wales Bull outside of Concord, Massachusetts, in 1849 from the native *Vitis labrusca* and, most likely, a Catawba, Bull planted some 22,000 seedlings before he had produced the grape that would own the jelly market, his cuttings eventually garnering him a tidy $1,000 apiece. However, riches ultimately eluded Bull, and his tombstone reads "He sowed—others reaped." Among those who reaped was Dr. Thomas Welch, who, in 1869 in appropriately named Vineland, New Jersey, boiled and sieved 40 pounds of 'Concord' grapes from his home arbor, and, employing the Pasteur method of sterilization, proceeded to bottle the world's first 12 quarts of fresh, unfermented grape juice. Dark blue to purple in hue and highly aromatic, 'Concord' is what is referred to as a "slip-skin" grape, meaning you can pop the translucent green flesh out of the skin and into your mouth just by giving it a squeeze. They grow on thick, woody vines lush with handsome green leaves and curling tendrils, and, a happily seedless variety, 'Concord Seedless,' developed by the New York Fruit Testing Station, has recently been made available.

Like all grapes, both of these varieties are an excellent source of potassium and antioxidants, and are known to stimulate the kidneys,

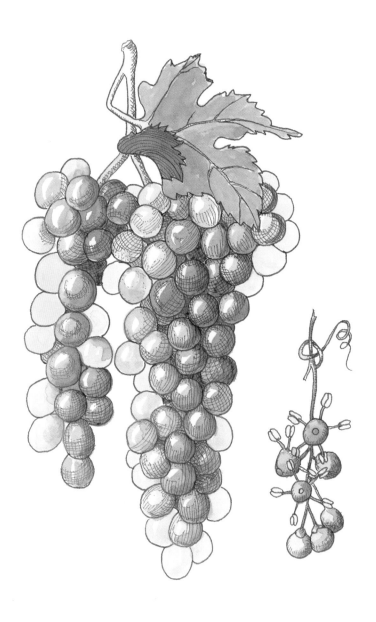

GRAPE 'NEPTUNE'

cleanse the liver, and neutralize uric acid. Both 'Neptune' and 'Concord Seedless' will do well in most any soil, and are hardy to USDA zone 5 (zone 4 for the nonseedless 'Concord' type), although all *labrusca* grapes, unlike the more resistant muscadines, will probably require several sprayings in a season for optimal cropping and disease prevention: again, your call entirely. Still, to be able to stand in the scented, green shade of your own grape arbor and to pop a fresh green 'Neptune' or squeeze a cooling morsel of tart/sweet 'Concord' flesh into your mouth on an August afternoon: well, just think about it.

33. Grapefruit 'Red Rio'
Citrus paradisii

*During the Great Depression, many people on food stamps encoun-
tered the grapefruit for the first time, and the Welfare Board was
besieged with complaints that they had cooked the unfamiliar fruit
for several hours and it was still too tough to eat.*

While there is no evidence of grapefruit trees growing natively
in the Old World or Asia, in the West Indies there are vast
populations of grapefruits growing seemingly wild.
Therefore, it is believed that the grapefruit as we know it was born there
in the eighteenth century, most probably as an accidental mating of the
pummelo (*Citrus grandis*) and the sweet orange (*Citrus sinensis*). The
pummelo, native to Malaysia and Indonesia, was delivered into the West
Indies from the Malay Archipelago by one Captain Shaddock, an English
ship commander, in 1693, becoming known alternately as the "shaddock."
The orange was introduced to the New World by Columbus on his second voyage in 1493, when he carried seeds into Hispaniola (Haiti). The
English reverend Griffith Hughes came upon either the pummelo or the
grapefruit in 1750 and, as he happened to be on a quest for the true identity of that pesky apple of Eden, decided to elect the large, yellowish,
West Indian thing upon which he had chanced, naming it the "forbidden
fruit," a name which followed both the pummelo and grapefruit around
for decades.

In 1820, the Chevalier de Tussac, a French botanist, reported from
Jamaica: "I have had the occasion to observe . . . a variety of shaddock
whose fruits . . . are disposed in clusters . . ." Somewhere along the line,
this "disposed in clusters" idea generated the grapefruit's present odd
sobriquet, as nothing could be less grapelike than a grapefruit. What we
now know as the grapefruit was delivered into Florida by Dr. Odette
Phillipi, a naval surgeon under Napoleon, who settled near Tampa in 1823
and developed the first American grapefruit grove there. The first pink

Grapefruit 'Red Rio'

grapefruit, 'Foster,' was discovered in Florida in 1907 as a renegade sport of the white-fleshed 'Walters' variety, and, in 1929, a Texas grower developed a red grapefruit on a pink grapefruit tree, naming it 'Ruby Red,' it ultimately becoming not only the first grapefruit ever granted a U.S. patent, but also the official state fruit of Texas in 1993. In 1971, 'Ruby Red' bud wood irradiated at the Brookhaven National Laboratory on Long Island eventually led to the creation of the 'Red Rio' grapefruit in 1976, and it is this lusciously red-fleshed variety I will recommend to you now.

Widely grown in Texas, more vigorous and hardy than its cousin 'Star Ruby' and sweeter than 'Ruby Red,' 'Red Rio' also achieves the added sparkle of a nearly seedless habit and, for those of us in nontropical zones, the ability to be "dwarfed" for pot culture. Like all red and pink grapefruits, 'Red Rio' shines with big doses of vitamins A and C, a host of B vitamins, calcium, potassium, and magnesium, and grapefruits, in general, are useful for stimulating digestion and their diuretic properties. 'Red Rio' should begin bearing about 4 years after planting and is capable of producing as many as 40 sweet/tart, pink-skinned, crimson-fleshed fruits per branch. A really lovely tree, adaptable to almost any soil, with large, shiny, ovate leaves, and fragrant white, four-petaled blossoms, 'Red Rio' would make a superb statement in your yard if you are in USDA zone 9 or above. For the rest of us, 'Red Rio,' with some energetic pruning, will do just fine in a 10-gallon pot to be hauled into the greenhouse or your sunniest window in winter. Why not whip up a tangy and colorful 'Red Rio' vinaigrette for your next salad by pureeing 1 cup chopped grapefruit flesh with 1/2 cup water, 1/4 cup cider vinegar, 4 tablespoons maple syrup, and salt and pepper to taste?

❧ 34. Greengage 'Denniston's Superb' ❧
Prunus domestica

"Little Jack Horner sat in the corner
Eating his Christmas pie,
He put in his thumb and pulled out a plum
And said 'What a good boy am I!' "

—Traditional English rhyme, eighteenth century

Let's get this "Little Jack Horner" thing out of the way first. "Jack," far from being exemplary, was actually one "Thomas" Horner, sixteenth-century steward to Richard Whiting, Catholic abbot of Glastonbury. In 1540, during Henry VIII's dissolution of the monasteries, Whiting sent Horner to London with a Christmas pie in which were concealed the deeds of a dozen manors, which the abbot hoped might assuage the newly Protestant monarch. On the journey, Horner extracted for himself the "plum" of the deed to the manor of Mells in Somerset, and betrayed the abbot to the king, Horner's family subsequently occupying Mells right into the twentieth century. A sixteenth-century rhyme commented: "Hopton, Horner, Smyth and Thynne: When Abbotts went out, they came in."

The actual "plum" antique to Europe is thought to be anciently original to Syria and Persia, although stones from the *Prunus domestica* have been unearthed at Maiden Castle in Dorset, England, dating to a very impressive eighth-century B.C. By the first century A.D., with over 300 identified varieties, Pliny the Elder noted: "no other tree has been so ingeniously crossed." The "European plum" entered the New World with the first seventeenth-century English settlers, and George Washington is known to have planted "three amber Plumbs . . . and 2 Green gage . . ." at Mount Vernon on February 27, 1786.

Greengages are historically thought to be the champagne of the *Prunus* family. Known continentally as *Reine Claude*, after the daughter of

GREENGAGE 'DENNISTON'S SUPERB'

Louis XII and consort of Francis I of France, greengages are actually believed to be of ancient Armenian extraction, were further cultured in France, and were imported into England in 1724, when Sir William Gage, Second Baronet of Hengrave, was sent seeds from the Chartreuse Monastery near Paris by his brother, the Reverend John Gage, which he planted at the family seat, Firle Place, near Bury St. Edmunds in Suffolk. Purportedly, the labels identifying the "Reine Claude" were lost in transit, and, as the fruits were "green" and he was "Gage," the "Greengage" was born. Renowned for their rich, intensely honeyed taste, the pretty yellow/green greengage is judged by food plant aficionados to be one of the most refined and exquisitely flavored fruits in existence, the most swoony identifying the flesh as both "nectar-like" and "ambrosial." In his *The Fruits and Fruit Trees of America* of 1845, A. J. Dowling waxes positively poetic: "The Green Gage is universally admitted to hold the first rank in flavour among all plums, and is every where highly esteemed . . ." with a "flavour, at once, sprightly and very luscious."

Needless to say, "Greengage" plums were a huge hit in the New World when first introduced, but, unfortunately, have since been overshadowed, by, shall we say, less demanding temperaments, for the unfortunate truth is, greengages are more prone to cracking and rot than other plums, have a higher winter chilling requirement, and tend to sporadic fruiting in warmer climes. On the other hand, they are pretty, smallish trees with copious, fragrant white blossoms in spring, are generally self-fertile, and are hardy to USDA zones 5 through 9. 'Denniston's Superb' greengage, with sweet, transparent flesh and a slight red blush, is probably the most generally available variety as well as the most reliable in terms of hardiness, self-fertility, and dependable cropping. And then there's that uniquely "ambrosial" flesh. And then the fact that all *Prunus domestica* types are beyond impressive in terms of their antioxidant performance, being particularly effective in neutralizing the notoriously destructive "superoxide anion" oxygen radical. I say what the hell: give one a try and hope to find a host of those heavenly fruits hanging nearby in about 5 years' time.

35. Hardy Kiwi 'Issai'
Actinidia arguta

Due to its usually fuzzy and diminutively evocative form, the French have attached the sobriquet "souris vegetale" to the kiwifruit, translating to "vegetable mouse."

The kiwifruit was born in the Yangtze River Valley of China, where, known as *Yang-tao*, it grew as wildly as kudzu does in the American South, girdling trees, swagging through forests, and, generally, growing so prolifically that the Chinese collected the fruit exclusively from the wild for several millennia. A member of the *Actinidiaceae* family, the kiwi has three main edible types: the small-fruited, smooth-skinned *A. chinensis;* the familiar, larger, fuzzy-skinned *A. deliciosa;* and *A. arguta*, the hardy kiwi. Also known as the "Bower Actinidia" and the "Tara Vine," the hardy kiwi, however antique to the Orient, was not exported outside China until 1904, when Isabel Fraser, headmistress of the Wanganui Girls' College in New Zealand, carried seeds home from her sister's mission, ultimately to be planted by Alexander Allison of Wanganui, New Zealand, where the vines first fruited in 1910.

In 1934, a kiwi vine introduced into the USDA Plant Introduction Station in Chico, California, thrived, becoming the single parent of the entire modern California kiwi industry, and, finally, in 1952, back in New Zealand, 13 tons of kiwifruit were exported to England, constituting the first-ever commercial shipment of a fruit so tardy, it did not even acquire its current appellation until the middle of the last century. Before that time, the kiwi was known near universally as the "Chinese gooseberry," until, in 1959, the Auckland fruit packers Turners & Growers decided to award the fruit the more enticing "melonette." That is, until they were apprised of the hefty import duties levied on melons, at which juncture they hopped right over to the Maori "kiwi," as the fruit was thought to resemble that round, brown native New Zealand bird.

Hardy Kiwi 'Issai'

Of course, by the 1970s, you couldn't lift the lid off a covered dish without discovering a slice or two of kiwi as the triumphant new *garni de jour*. Certainly, this constitutes just deserts, as the kiwi is one of the most nutritionally dense fruits in existence, with immense potential in lowering both cholesterol and stress and fighting cancer, as the kiwi is loaded with antioxidants, twice the vitamin C of an orange, 20 percent more potassium than a banana, and nice amounts of vitamin E, folic acid, and fiber. The University of Oslo reported that eating 2 to 3 kiwis a day will reduce blood clotting by an average of 18 percent and lower your triglycerides by an average of 15 percent, and the renowned Rowett Research Institute in England found that your DNA repair rate nearly doubles with the consumption of kiwifruit.

Therefore, we must all rejoice at the introduction of the hardy kiwi 'Issai,' which allows all of us to grow some of these emerald-fleshed bundles of nutrients. Not only is 'Issai' one of the hardiest kiwis, but it is also one of the few that is self-fertile, so you will only need one to achieve enormous yields of sweet, juicy, grape-sized, fuzzless fruit, borne in threes, with seeds as tiny as a strawberry's. 'Issai' will coil about your accommodating arbor or trellising, potentially growing to 15 feet in a season, with large, slightly serrated shiny green leaves and lovely 1- to 2-inch, white-mellowing-to-gold blossoms. Full sun and good drainage will be all you need to keep 'Issai' happy, as they are wonderfully pest-free, and genuinely hardy to USDA zones 4 through 9. The vines are decidedly "vigorous," and some pruning and tying up will keep your glorious, jungle-like tangle within its prescribed confines, although a certain wildness of habit does become it, and you will harvest bowls full of these succulent "pop-in-your-mouth" grape-sized fruits. I recommend halving a bunch and tossing with sliced avocado, raddichio, endive, some shrimp, and a fruity vinaigrette as a perfect late summer lunch.

❊ 36. Honeyberry ❊
Lonicera caerulea v. *edulis* (*Lonicera kamchatika*)

One of the interesting side benefits of glasnost (political openness),
which marked the restructuring of the Soviet Empire in 1986, was
the introduction of the Russian-bred honeyberry to the world.

Be prepared to greet the next big thing. Although honeyberries are not currently commercially available, many fruit growers are convinced that this comely and tasty berry will be the broadly feted darling of both supermarkets and nurseries in the next decade. Highly valued in its native habitat of Transbaikalia, the mountainous region east of Lake Baikal in Russia, and in Japan, where is it known as *Haskap*, this "blue" member of the honeysuckle family was first mentioned as a food plant of interest in 1894. Champions of this sprightly berry decided its honeysuckle roots would impede commercial popularity, and so the *Lonicera caerulea* v. *edulis* ("edible blue honeysuckle") was rechristened "honeyberry" around the turn of the twentieth century. Not to be confused with either the Old World hackberry (*Celtis australis*) or the West Indian Spanish lime (*Melicocca bijuga*), both also known as "honeyberry," *L. caerulea* v. *edulis* is the only member of the "blue honeysuckle" clan that is edible. Although there are some eighteenth- and nineteenth-century references to an "edible, early-ripening wild berry resembling a blueberry" in Russian and Japanese texts, the historically "closed" societies of both of those nations, and particularly the Soviet Union in the twentieth century, made dissemination of any information concerning the development of the edible honeyberry extremely late in coming.

We know the first attempts to domesticate the honeyberry in Russia date to about 1913; however, really extensive work did not commence until the 1950s, when the Vasilov Research Institute in St. Petersburg and the Siberian Horticultural Institute in Barnaul plunged into honeyberry hybridization with a good amount of attention. It appears the *Lonicera caerulea*'s most promising breeding cultivars hailed from the Kamchatka

HONEYBERRY

Peninsula of Russia (thus *Lonicera kamchatika*, the honeyberry's alternate botanical name), and collecting missions by the Vasilov Research Institute, conducted from 1972 to 1990, ultimately identified some 500 different edible honeyberry types. The first three Russian hybrids to hit the market, 'Start,' *'Goluboye vereteno,'* and *'Sinyaya Ptitsa,'* were released in 1980, and, by 1998, the number of viable commercial cultivars offered for sale in Russia had grown to 60. As well, culture of the *Haskap* in Japan, primarily on the island of Hokkaido, has yielded a booming modern commercial industry. Visually (and, most feel, culinarily) akin to the blueberry, the honeyberry does, in fact, resemble an elongated blueberry, dented at the nether end, the berries produced on compact, 5-foot shrubs in easy-to-harvest clusters, and each berry containing not only a tiny edible seed, but a significant (think blueberry-like) load of antioxidants as well.

As you might expect from their points of origin, honeyberries are mightily hardy to -40 degrees F (USDA zone 3), and, even more impressive, honeyberries typically require only one growing season to fruit, and the fruit is produced exceptionally early—about 2 weeks before the first strawberries appear. In terms of cultivar, there seems to be a "blue" theme running through the most popular, with 'Blue Belle,' 'Blue Bird,' 'Blue Forest,' 'Blue Moon,' 'Blue Pacific,' and 'Blue Velvet' leading the pack, all offering attractive dark green foliage followed by delicate yellow/white flowers in summer, with the deep blue berries arriving in early fall, followed by very vivacious golden fall foliage. Honeyberries are also nicely uncomplaining in terms of soil preference, drought tolerance, pest issues, etc., but are not self-fertile, so they will require at least 2 varieties and some cross-pollination to fruit successfully. Some people feel the honeyberry tastes of blueberry infused with black currant: employ them deliciously every way you would a blueberry, including over your cereal at breakfast time, and have something horticulturally cutting edge to chat about at dinner.

⚜ 37. Huckleberry (Bilberry) ⚜
Vaccinium sp. / *Gaylussacia* sp.

According to The Guinness Book of Records, *the world's oldest living thing is a "box huckleberry" in Perry County, Pennsylvania, a single plant spreading underground for almost a mile and being believed to date to the eleventh century B.C.*

This is the story of a fruit that simply cannot make up its mind, as there are "huckleberries" belonging to 3 entirely different genera, *Solanaceae* ("garden huckleberry"), *Vaccinium* ("bilberry," "huckleberry," "farkleberry," "whortleberry"), and that *Vaccinium* cousin in the greater *Ericaceae* family, *Gaylussacia* ("black huckleberry," "box huckleberry," "dwarf huckleberry"). The "garden huckleberry," a relation of Deadly Nightshade, is entirely toxic and should be shunned outright. The related *Vaccinium* and *Gaylussacia* types boast both edible and nonedible varieties, a good number of which, as referenced, are called "huckleberry," or some antique variation thereof ("whortleberry," "bilberry," "farkleberry," and so on). And, just to add one more stumbling block to this testy tale, in the United States, the edible *Vaccinium* types are native only to the Pacific Northwest, while the edible *Gaylussacias* are native to eastern America alone.

Both wild *Vacciniums* and *Gaylussacias* (named for the nineteenth-century French physicist Joseph Louis Gay-Lussac) were an antique and important food source for a host of Native American tribes, Henry David Thoreau recounting that ". . . from time immemorial . . . [Native Americans] have made far more extensive use of the whortleberry at all seasons and in various ways than we . . . ." The first non-Native mention of the huckleberry seems to occur in the diaries of Samuel de Champlain in 1615, who noted that the Algonquins collected and dried them, and, in 1624, the Franciscan missionary Gabriel Sagard related that the Hurons of the Great Lakes ". . . regularly dry them for the winter . . . and that serves them for comfits for the sick." The term "huckleberry" first

Huckleberry (Bilberry)

appears in *The History of Carolina* by John Lawson, the surveyor general of that state, in 1709, deriving from "hurtleberry," a corruption of the ancient Saxon *Heart-berg* ("Hart's berry"). Huckleberries were an important part of Lewis and Clark's diet in 1805 and 1806, and, in 1868, Robert Brown, Scottish explorer of the Pacific Northwest, wrote of the scores of huckleberry cakes that could be seen drying in Native American villages "supervised by some ancient hag, whose hands and arms are dyed pink with them."

As mentioned, *Vaccinium* huckleberries are native only to the western United States and *Gaylussacias* to the East. In general, the *Gaylussacia* huckleberries are hardier (about zones 4 to 9), but the most common varieties, "dwarf," "box," "blue," and "black," are such touchy transplants and so readily available in the wild that they are virtually undomesticated. As for the *Vacciniums*, they are mostly only hardy to zones 7 through 9, although adaptable in terms of sun and siting, and have interesting landscape potential. Here I will pause to bandy a few types about: *V. myrtillus*, native to both North America and Europe, is a handsome 2-foot bush, bearing flavorful 1/4-inch black, purple, or dark blue berries; *V. caespitosum* is a wonderful ground cover growing to about 1 foot with small, bright blue berries with excellent flavor; and *V. ovatum*, particularly the 'Thunderbird' variety, has a handsome upright habit to about 6 feet, especially attractive new red/bronze foliage, and tasty dark blue fruit that is both larger and bluer than most other types. All huckleberries of either genus, like all deep blue/black fruits, are loaded with healthful anthocyanins.

Would I honestly encourage you to plant a huckleberry? Let us put it this way: if you can make a 'Thunderbird' work in your environment, they are awfully decorative and are an especially pretty foil for laurels and rhododendrons in a wet woodland setting. If not, there is undoubtedly some huckleberry or other growing wild in your precincts. Go taste one (not the *Solanum* variety!) and see if it is worth considering picking a bunch and stuffing them under a pie crust.

❦ 38. Jujube 'So' ❦
Ziziphus zizyphus

"Then came Jesus forth, wearing the crown of thorns, and the purple robe. And Pilate saith unto them, Behold the man!"

—John 19:5

The genus *Ziziphus* contains about 40 species native to temperate and subtropical parts of the Old World, the edible types most notably including the Chinese jujube, *Z. zizyphus*, the Middle Eastern *Z. spinachristi*, the Mediterranean *Z. lotus*, and the Indian/West African *Z. mauretanica*. Although it is the Chinese type we will be generally discussing here, allow me to digress briefly in the direction of the Middle Eastern *Z. spinachristi*, or 'Christ Thorn' jujube, so named because many botanists believe it was the literal "thorn" in the crown worn by Jesus on his journey to Golgotha. Considered anciently sacred in both Israel and Islam, in Israel it was believed that when a jujube tree reached an age of 40 years, the saints would congregate beneath it. *Z. zizyphus*, also known as the "Chinese date" or *Tsao*, is a small deciduous tree thought to be originally native to Syria, although it has grown in China for over 4,000 years and is chiefly identified with that country.

Universally judged the tastiest as well as the hardiest of the edible *Ziziphus* clan, the Chinese jujube is famously lauded in the *Shi Jing* or "Classic of Odes," the first anthology of Chinese poetry dating to the fifth century B.C. In ancient China, jujubes were prescribed as a general "rejuvenator" of those suffering from illness or stress and, in a nice case of parallel employment, Pakistan and India antiquely prescribed jujubes as a near-panacea for strength, stamina, and disease prevention. The Greek botanist Theophrastus, referring to the 'Christ Thorn" jujube in the fourth century B.C., noted: "the fruit is . . . round and red, and in size as large as the fruit of the prickly cedar or a little larger . . . but the fruit is sweet. . . ." By the seventeenth century, English herbalist John Gerard was recommending the jujube as an excellent tonic for all parts of the

Jujube 'So'

body. It is believed that the first jujube in North America arrived with one Robert Chisolm via Beaufort, North Carolina, in 1837, although they are also mentioned in relation to some of the earliest Spanish missions in California.

Jujube fruit, which can actually be olive- to plum-sized and of various colorations, depending on phase, goes through a number of interesting physical stages: first green-skinned, white-fleshed, and crunchy and sweet as an apple; then through a softer, yellowish, maroon-spotted phase; and finally turning a rich purple/red and wrinkling up like a date, which it closely resembles in both form and taste (thus "Chinese date"). Jujube trees are lovely, gracefully gnarled, drooping things, typically growing to 10 to 20 feet with shiny, leathery, bright green leaves and tiny yellow-green flowers. As well, jujubes seem to thrive on neglect, be untroubled by pests, and are self-fertile, although fruit and yield will be increased with cross-pollination. The only slight glitch is, being of a temperate to subtropical nature, they will thrive best in hot, dry climates, and most are hardy only to USDA zone 6.

Therefore, while the varieties 'Li' and 'Lang,' both developed by Frank Meyer of 'Meyer Lemon' fame, are very popular for both habit and fruit quality, here I will recommend to you the semidwarf, perfect-for-pot-culture variety 'So,' also known as the "Contorted jujube." A tree of uniquely beautiful shape, especially with both twigs and leaves fallen in the winter, every node of every branch of 'So' creates a new angle, forming a truly inspirational take on the distinctive "zigzag" silhouette for which jujubes are so notable. Every jujube variety will have a preferred stage of edibility, 'So' being wonderful at the green/yellow stage and fresh off the tree, while others are better consumed at a later crimson or dried moment, 'So' choose your type, and start sampling . . . You won't regret it.

❦ 39. Kumquat 'Fukushu' ❦
Fortunella obovata

"Here's the thing. If you put a single kumquat on the scale, it doesn't even register. It's so light. So light. The word is almost heavier."

—Rob Hardy,
"Kumquat," *Plum Ruby Review*, February 2004

The kumquat is the smallest member of the *Citrus* clan, and is unique in two ways. First, it is the only *Citrus* fruit with an edible rind. Second, it is both sweet *and* tart, with, oddly, the edible rind being the sweet element and the flesh, in most varieties, being the acidic component. For these and several other proprietary genetic traits, kumquats were removed from the *Citrus* family in 1915 and given their own genus, *Fortunella,* by USDA plant physiology chief Dr. Walter T. Swingle, who named it for the British plant explorer Robert Fortune, who introduced the kumquat to Europe from China in 1846. Native to eastern Asia and Malaysia, the fruit's name "kumquat" derives from the early Cantonese *kin kü*, which translates to "golden orange." The first literary depiction of the kumquat appears in the early Chinese botanist Han Yen-Chih's *Chu lu* of 1178 A.D., and the kumquat's first European mention occurs in the Italian Jesuit Giovanni Battista Ferrari's treatise, *Hesperides sive de Malorum Aureorum Cultura* of 1646, in which he refers to the "Aurantium . . . minuscule '*Kin kiu*'" from information supplied by the Portuguese missionary Alvarus Semedus, who had discovered it in China.

Current popular varieties include the ancient 'Hong Kong' kumquat (*F. hindsii*), thought to be the wild ancestor of the lot, the round 'Marumi' (*F. japonica*), the 'Meiwa' (*F. crassifolia*), favored in the Orient, the oval 'Nagami' (*F. margarita*), the one typically found dotting holiday fruit baskets, and the 'Fukushu' (*F. obovata*), the type I will recommend here. Also known as the 'Changshou' kumquat, which translates to "longevity," the species *Fortunella obovata* was established by the Japanese botanist Tanaka in 1933, and I recommend it to you because it is

KUMQUAT 'FUKUSHU'

the kumquat with the most successful dwarf habit as well as the thinnest rind, making it perfect for pot culture for those of us in less-than-temperate zones and excellent for fresh consumption. However, the 'Meiwa' and the 'Nagami' types are also both entirely commendable in habit and fruit quality and, if zone and plant size are not an issue, I would not hesitate to point you in their direction.

Kumquats will usually grow to about 10 to 12 feet, but the 'Fukushu,' habitually grown on *Poncirus trifoliata* rootstock, can be kept dwarfed to only 4 or 5 feet. Additionally, it is a supremely ornamental tree with a tight yet spreading habit, signature glossy *Citrus* foliage and heavenly white blossoms, and charmingly copious, oval, brilliant orange, inch-and-a-half-long fruit. The 'Fukushu' should be hardy down to the low 20s F (USDA zone 9a), and possibly to even lower temperatures if they are brief. For the rest of us, I'll pause to reiterate the infinite appeal of pot culture: there is simply nothing so blissful in the doldrums of February or March as the gloss and green and scent of any *Citrus* tree in a big terracotta pot. If you can have one, do. If you can have a pair, all the better.

Kumquats are an excellent source of vitamins A and C, are cholesterol, fat, and sodium free, and offer fiber, calcium, and iron to boot. With their sweet edible rinds and tart flesh, the 'Fukushu' would be perfect for the very pretty hostess gift of a jar of preserved kumquats. Slit 4 quarts of them with a deep "x" at each blossom end, cover with water and simmer for 10 minutes till tender and translucent. In a separate pot, boil 3 cups each water and sugar until syrupy (about 10 minutes), add kumquats, simmer for 20 minutes, pack in sterilized jars, and gift to some lucky gourmet.

☙

40. Lemon 'Meyer' (Improved)
Citrus limon

". . . you spill a universe of gold
a yellow goblet of miracles
a fragrant nipple of the Earth's breast . . ."

—Pablo Neruda, "Ode to a Lemon," 2005

Certainly the lemon is originally native to the Far and/or Middle East, with various claques championing Malaysia, Myanmar, China, and India as its birthplace. A "lemon-shaped" earring found in Malaysia, dating to 2500 B.C., has made Malaysia the site *du jour*, but that shape could also accurately describe the citron and the lime, so the debate rages on. Additionally, some, like the Israeli historian S. Tolkowsky, believe lemons were known in Italy as early as 300 A.D., as a mosaic floor dating to second-century Carthage displays recognizable lemons, while others identify the Carthaginian image as a citron and have the lemon entering Italy in the eleventh century with the returning Crusaders. As all *Citrus* were also essentially lumped historically into one great vat of fragrantly flowered juice, this clearly remains a huge gray (if tartly flavored) area.

What seems beyond debate is that, by the end of the fifteenth century, the infamous Cesare Borgia was sending gifts of lemons and oranges to his wife in France, John Gerard notes both *limons* and *orenges* in use in England in his *Herball* of 1636, and, by the end of the seventeenth century, Louis XIV was bestowing tokens of oranges and lemons upon his royal favorites, who apparently employed them to "redden their lips," which I can only imagine must have entailed a very brisk rubbing. The lemon was introduced to the New World by Christopher Columbus in 1493, and by the mid-sixteenth century, the Spanish missionary Bartolomé de las Casas noted them growing in the West Indies. Most botanists place introduction into North America via Florida at some moment between 1513, when Ponce de León arrived in search of his

Lemon 'Meyer' (Improved)

fountain of youth, and 1565, when St. Augustine, the first Floridian colony, was established.

With all this fascinating provenance related, you have undoubtedly caught on to the fact that the lemon is native to thickly warm climates and, therefore, is hardy only in USDA zones 8b to 10, which will make perennial culture decidedly difficult for a good number of you. Therefore, here I will bring the curtain up on that diminutive, eminently pot-cultivable darling the Lemon 'Meyer' (Improved). Apparently known in China since the fourteenth century and thought to be a cross between a lemon and a mandarin orange, the first 'Meyer' in the U.S. was carried into California from Beijing in 1908 by Frank N. Meyer, a U.S. government botanist, and subsequently named for him. Unfortunately, this original 'Meyer' was prone to the *Citrus tristeza* virus, which was troublesome to other *Citrus* varieties, until it was "improved" in the mid-1950s by Don Dillon, Sr., son of pioneering dwarf *Citrus* hybridizer Floyd Dillon, founder of White Winds Growers in Fremont, California, when he discovered a virus-free clone in their test fields. All Lemon 'Meyer' Improved plants propagated in California to this day derive from that single "improved" mother tree.

The 'Meyer' is not only beautifully compact in habit, certainly capable of being kept to 8 feet or under depending on your pruning preferences and the size of your pot, but also self-fruitful, admirably unfinicky, and notoriously prolific, often flowering twice a year. The 'Meyer' piles on a few more laurels with the addition of lush, glossy green leaves and intensely fragrant white flowers, but it is its ruddy golden fruits that are the real treasure, notable for their unique lemon/orange taste, juicy amplitude, and thick, admirably candy-able and zest-able rind. Just give your 'Meyer' a healthy dose of sun and water, indoors and out, roll indoors when temperatures hit below 30 degrees, rotate occasionally, and you will be rewarded all year long on all kinds of matchless sensory levels.

✦ 41. Lime 'Key Lime' ✦
Citrus aurantifolia

Between 1795 and 1815, after it was discovered that scurvy could be cured with liberal doses of lime juice, some 1.6 million gallons of it were consumed by British sailors, giving birth to the sobriquet "limey."

Citrus plants, in general, are antiquely native to India, the Malay Archipelago, and the Far East (think 4000 B.C.). Sweet oranges probably originated in India, the trifoliate oranges and mandarins in China, and the tarter citrus types, including the key lime, in Malaysia. However, some taxonomists feel that the prehistoric antecedent of the entire clan may be the *Microcitrus*, a tall, small-fruited rainforest tree native only to northeastern Australia, and so unbelievably ancient that it probably grew before the continents of Australia and Asia drifted apart. Like many originally subtropical fruits, the key lime, believed to have both *Microcitrus*, the grapefruit-like pummelo (*Citrus grandis*), and the citron (*Citrus medica*) in its parentage, made its way into North Africa and Arabia along the spice roads, and was finally imported into the southern Mediterranean in the fourth century B.C., probably with the returning legions of Alexander the Great. From the second century B.C. onward, *Citrus* groves were founded all over southern Europe, and potted specimens, which could be carted into greenhouses, popularly dotted European parterres from the fifteenth century onward.

Columbus is credited with delivering the key lime to Hispaniola (now Haiti) in 1493, from whence it was carried to Florida by Spanish settlers at the turn of the sixteenth century. The key lime found an especially happy home in the tropical climes of the south Florida Keys and, shortly after the turn of the twentieth century, farmers there abandoned their commercial pineapple crop in its favor, thus giving birth to the "Key" lime's current appellation. However, in 1926, the Great Miami Hurricane decimated the lime groves of the Keys, which were never to be restored. Today, Mexico is the world's largest producer of key limes. Clearly, being

LIME 'KEY LIME'

a truly tropical cultivar, the lime will not be hardy below USDA zones 9–10, and it is therefore the key lime I recommend to you here, as it is another excellent and very appealing candidate for pot culture.

A semidwarf tree with glossy green leaves and very fragrant, tiny white flowers preceding fruit, the key lime is both a rapid grower and easily prunable to your preferred habit. And it will produce heavily even when young. The fruit of the key lime (*Citrus aurantifolia*) is much smaller than that of its far more ubiquitous cousin, the Persian lime (*Citrus latifolia*), nearly spherical versus the Persian lime's more zeppelin-like shape, and thinner of skin. Interestingly, key limes are really only ripe when they turn yellow (and their pronounced tartness mellows to something approaching sweetness): green key limes are actually immature fruits, although equally prized for their tart punch. A key lime cultured in a container will be blissfully happy out on your terrace in a nice sunny position when temperatures remain above 60 degrees, and will do splendidly indoors in a sunny spot in winter in the same temperature range. In any season, water thoroughly when the soil appears dry, keeping in mind, however, that all *Citrus* plants like a period of dryness in between waterings, giving the root system a nice shot of beneficial oxygen. I believe it would be heartless for me to offer up anything less than the "Heirloom Key Lime Pie" recipe suggested by the *Key West Cook Book* of 1949. Therefore, make or buy a graham cracker crust. Then beat 4 egg yolks until light, and whisk in one can sweetened condensed milk, 1/2 cup key lime juice, and 1/2 teaspoon cream of tartar. Spoon into your crust and bake at 325 degrees until set (10 to 15 minutes). Refrigerate for 3 hours and serve to your adoring multitude, with or without a topping of baked meringue.

🎄 42. Lingonberry (Cowberry) 🎄
Vaccinium vitis-idaea

The lingonberry was so vital a food source in ancient Scandinavia that, in Iceland, thirteenth-century law decreed that the number of berries you could pick on land not your own was limited to what you could consume on the spot.

The lingonberry, also known as the cowberry, fox berry, mountain cranberry, partridgeberry, and red whortleberry, is a small evergreen shrub of the *Ericaceae* family, which grows wild in the mountainous regions of Scandinavia, Russia, Canada, and—in the United States—Maine. The remains of lingonberry wine found in ancient Danish graves indicates human consumption as far back as the Bronze Age (1800–600 B.C.), and lingonberries are as much of a fruit staple in Scandinavia as are their *Vaccinium* cousin blueberries and cranberries in North America. A near ringer for the cranberry, lingonberries, with their glossy, bright red fruit and neat, small-scale leaves, are preferred by many not only for their sweeter taste, but also for their exceedingly decorative habit. In fact, in 1651, André Mollet, French gardener to Sweden's Queen Christina, recommended in his *Le Jardin de Plaisir* that the lingonberry be employed for the edging of parterre gardens rather than the traditional box.

It was Lorenzo Magalotti, editor of the *Saggi di Naturali Esperienze*, who wrote the first European account of the lingonberry following a trip to Sweden in 1674, and the lingonberry figures heavily in Christian Gartner's *Hortikultura* of 1694, which recommended it for both culinary and herbal usage. Carl Linnaeus had identified the lingonberry by 1748, they were included by the Swedish economist Johan Fischerstrom in his dictionary of natural science of 1779, and Jahan Anders Retzius, the Swedish botanist and entomologist, wrote glowingly of them in his tome on economically useful plants of 1806. Aside from being, as noted, a striking ornamental plant, the lingonberry, according to Retzius, was

LINGONBERRY (COWBERRY)

excellent for fever patients, enjoyed historic employment as an anti-scorbutic and diarrhea medication, and tea brewed from the lingon-berry's leaf was recommended for both rheumatism and urinary tract infections. Additionally, the lingonberry could be stored almost indefi-nitely, the traditional method, again according to Retzius, being conser-vation in water-filled jars.

Yet with all these sterling attributes plus an iron constitution, being hardy in USDA zones 2 through 8, the lingonberry has, tragically, never really caught on outside its native habitat. This is a distinct loss for home gardeners as the lingonberry is one of the prettiest ground cover ideas going: an ornamental triple threat of pretty flower, gorgeous fruit, and handsome leaf and habit, growing to a delightfully compact 8 to 10 inches. Planted in a mass, lingonberries, although conveniently self-fruitful, are spectacular as a thick carpet of finely-wrought foliage, robust even in the bitterest cold, and dotted with pretty pink-blushed, bell-shaped white flowers in spring and sparkling vermillion fruit in fall. As mentioned, lingonberry plants are rather difficult to find, so I will not recommend just one type here, although some of the most popular varieties are 'Sussi,' the very first lingonberry to be selected and named; 'Regal,' developed at the University of Wisconsin from Finnish seed; 'Masovia;' and 'Koralle.'

All are hardy in the extreme, will prefer some shade in zones 6 to 8, and insist on soil on the acidic side (pH 3.5 to 5). Plants can be slow to establish and will require some attention to weeding, mulching, and watering during the first couple of seasons, so have a bit of patience. Their fine flavor aside, lingonberries are chockablock with vitamins B and C, beta-carotene, and other cancer-fighting anthocyanins, as well as healthy amounts of potassium, calcium, magnesium, and phosphorus, so employ these berries, cooked and sweetened, exactly as you would a cranberry: in preserves, sauces for both desserts and meats, pie fillings, relishes, and so on. *Nota bene*: lingonberry preserves as an accompani-ment to homemade Swedish meatballs and mashed potatoes is a treat you would be wise not to miss.

❧ 43. Loquat ❧
Eriobotrya japonica

"Brown streaky house finch
Your crest as orange as loquats
Ripe fruit and peeping."

—Rana, "Loquat Season," 2005

The loquat, a *Prunus* half-brother to the kumquat, is indigenous to southeastern China, where it is commonly called *pipa*, after the Chinese lute, whose shape it is thought to resemble. The loquat was mentioned frequently in ancient Chinese literature, most notably in the eighth-century A.D. verses of the great poet Li Bai, who, legend has it, drowned in the Yangtze River while trying to drunkenly embrace the moon's reflection. In Chinese lore, the loquat, perhaps because of its downy, blushing skin and sweet, pale flesh, is linked with courtesans, a brothel being antiquely referred to as a "gate of loquats." Loquats have grown in Japan since around 1100 A.D., where they were called *biwa*, also after a lutelike instrument, and the German botanist Engelbert Kaempfer, sent to Deshima off the coast of Nagasaki, Japan, by the Dutch East India Company in 1690, was the first European to describe the loquat.

The loquat had been planted in the French National Gardens in Paris by 1784 and in the Royal Botanical Gardens at Kew by 1787. By 1818, "Japanese medlars," so named because of their familial resemblance to the native European type (*Mespilus germanica*), were being produced in hothouses throughout Europe. By the mid-nineteenth century, the loquat was commonplace in California and, by the turn of the twentieth, firmly established throughout the southern United States, where it is commonly known as the "Japanese" or "Chinese plum." Medicinally, the loquat boasts substantial quantities of vitamins A and C, calcium, potassium, phosphorus, and iron, and, like most *Prunus* descendants, the seeds

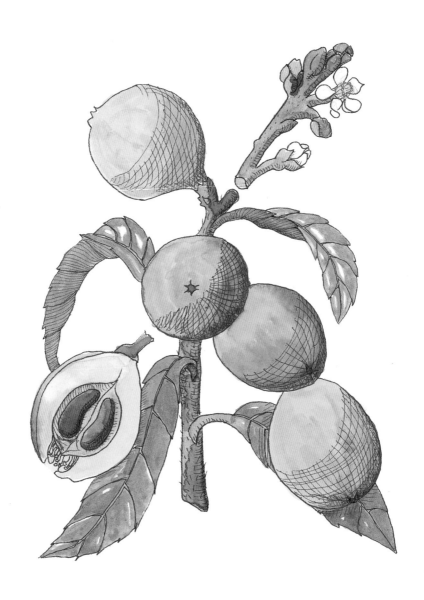

Loquat

and young leaves contain cyanogenic glycocides, which, in limited doses, are the active elements in the experimental cancer drug Laetrile. In Japan, drinking loquat leaf tea and ingesting 2 seeds per day has proven highly successful in combating liver and pancreatic cancer, the seeds being 1,300 times higher in laetrile than the leaves.

A small tree, usually growing to 10 to 20 feet, loquats are true mavericks among fruit trees as, in our climate, their flowers will not appear till fall, and the fruit will not ripen until late winter. Therefore, the loquat will only fruit in areas where winters remain very mild indeed (consistently above 30 degrees F), and is only hardy to USDA zone 8 and above. Handily, the loquat is another prime candidate for pot culture: a handsome ornamental that offers large, waxy, beautifully veined, dark green leaves with a woolly underside (much like a magnolia leaf), and small, white, sweetly fragrant flowers. Loquat fruits grow in clusters, can be oval, rounded, or pear-shaped, with the flesh deep orange, yellow, or white, and smooth or downy of skin, depending on type. Each fruit contains 3 to 5 large brown seeds, and the fruit's flavor, at its best, has been compared to a rich, sweet blend of apricot, plum, and cherry.

There are over 800 varieties of loquat in the Orient, but I will not stop to recommend just one. What I will urge you to do is find one that is merely self-fertile if there is a chance of it fruiting in your yard, and one that is both self-fertile and grown on dwarfed rootstock if you plan to grow it in a pot, 'Gold Nugget' and 'Mogi' being two of the most popular self-fertile varieties. Loquats reach maturity about 90 days from flowering and should be allowed to ripen fully on the tree, when they will be perfect for fresh eating or a piquant loquat chutney. For that, boil together 3 pounds of loquats, stemmed, seeded, and chopped, 1 cup brown sugar, 2/3 cup cider vinegar, and 1 tablespoon each minced fresh ginger and grated orange peel, until thick and syrupy, about 45 minutes. Serve winningly hot or cold.

🎄 44. Magnolia Vine 'Eastern Prince' 🎄
Schisandra chinensis

The Chinese name for their esteemed magnolia vine, Wu wei zi, *translates to "five-flavored seed," as the fruit is said to be sweet, sour, bitter, pungent, and salty—all in one bite.*

Schisandra chinensis, also known as Schizandra, *Wu wei zi*, Fruit of Five Flavors, sandra berry, and, most commonly, the magnolia vine, is a food plant with absolutely everything going for it: a gorgeous, perennial vining habit, handsome foliage, stunning blossom, beautiful fruit, and health benefits literally from stem to stern, with leaves, roots, shoots, stems, and fruits all being important herbal ingredients. A cousin of the magnolia tree and anciently native to China, Japan, Russia, and Korea, the magnolia vine is considered to be one of the 50 fundamental plants of Traditional Chinese Medicine, its first herbal usage being recorded in the *Divine Husbandman's Materia Medica*, the earliest extant Chinese pharmacopoeia, believed to have been written by the emperor Shen Nung, "Shen Nung" translating to "Divine Husbandman." Myth holds this legendary figure, credited with being the father of both Chinese agriculture and medicine, and the inventor of the cart, the plow, and the first cup of tea, was born with the head of a bull and the body of a man around 2800 B.C.

The magnolia vine is Traditional Chinese Medicine's ultimate "balancing" herb, imparting the energy of the world's 5 distinct flavors at once, and, unusually, is represented as possessing qualities of both yin *and* yang. For thousands of years, *Schisandra* has been cherished as a kind of all-purpose rejuvenator, energizer, destresser, increaser of stamina and mental clarity, and sexual tonic, in the *Divine Husbandman's Materia Medica* it being said to "prolong the years of life without aging," and to add immeasurably to one's *qi* ("chee"), or personal energy. Also known as the "smart herb," *Schisandra* is believed to sharpen mental ability and concentration, while normalizing *qi* during times of stress; combating

Magnolia Vine 'Eastern Prince'

aging; acting as a kind of herbal Viagra; helping to relieve chronic gastritis, heartburn, and indigestion; producing glutathione peroxidase, which derails several types of free radicals; and offering a whopping 7 to 10 times as much vitamin C per ounce as an orange. Needless to say, you should have some.

Magnolia vine is still rather an oddity in non-Oriental parts, 'Eastern Prince' being the most generally available type, as well as being a model of beauty, vigor, pest-resistance, self-fertility, and hardiness to USDA zone 4, and, therefore, the one with which I will romance you here. 'Eastern Prince' will easily grow 10 to 20 feet in a season, so you will need to supply an ample arbor; its fragrant, beautifully magnolia-like, cream-blushed-with-pink blossoms appear in spring, nestled in a pretty ruff of green and white variegated leaves. In summer, 'Eastern Prince' will delight you with attractive green, slightly heart-shaped leaves running in threes along the vines, followed in early autumn by copious grapelike clusters of glossy vermilion berries, and climaxing in late fall with the foliage turning a brilliant gold before dropping.

'Eastern Prince,' as noted, is widely adaptable to a variety of soil types, as well to full sun or part shade, seems untroubled by pests or birds, and will begin fruiting about 3 years from planting. Regular fertilizing will help 'Eastern Prince' fruit faster and, although this regal food plant is frost-hardy, a bit of mulch on its crown will be appreciated when temperatures dip below 25 degrees F. In terms of consumption, the berries, as noted, are dried and ground for herbal usage, or may be crushed or juiced and sweetened for use in teas, tonics, jellies, and pies, and the leaves make an extremely healthful herbal tea. My advice? Grow one, dry some berries, steep a teaspoon or two in a mug, and make a dose of magnolia vine tea part of every day. It couldn't hurt.

❧ 45. Medlar 'Nottingham' ❧
Mespilus germanica

Due to the medlar's, shall we say, visually suggestive physiognomy, it was known with ancient charm in England as "open-arse," and in antique France as "cul de chien" (dog's ass).

The medlar (*Mespilus germanica*), yet another member of the greater order *Rosaceae*, is believed to be originally native to the western coast of the Caspian Sea, although inter-glacial impressions of medlar leaves in what was formerly eastern Germany point to incredible antiquity there as well. Archilochos of Paros, inventor of iambic poetic structure, noted them in Greece in about 650 B.C., and Theophrastus observed 3 varieties in his *History of Plants* of the third century B.C. Charlemagne recommended that medlars be planted in his Imperial Gardens around the turn of the ninth century A.D., and, in the same century, they were represented in the medicinal and culinary plant list of Switzerland's famous St. Galler Klostergardens. Aside from its edible and herbal qualities, the medlar was also historically esteemed for its exceptionally hard wood, which was employed in the manufacture of spear points, clubs, and fighting sticks, as well as, in northern Europe, the turning wheels of windmills.

The medlar maintained broad popularity in Europe from the Late Middle Ages right to the end of the nineteenth century, when it basically tumbled into gastronomic obscurity. In part, this is due to its rather controversial physiognomy, looking for all the world like a crabapple into which someone has inserted a small explosive, resulting in a rather provocative opening sporting a tattered skirt, the English garden writer J. C. Woodsford calling it in 1939: "a crabby-looking, brownish-green, truncated, little spheroid of unsympathetic appearance." The medlar's ultimate stumbling block, however, was of a more cultural description, as, unlike any other fruit, it must be picked when hard and green, and then "bletted," i.e., stored in a cool, dry place until its interior "ripens,"

Medlar 'Nottingham'

transforming itself from a hard ivory-fleshed novelty to a deflated, frankly suspect-looking brownish curiosity.

D. H. Lawrence declared them "wineskins of brown morbidity" for this cultural eccentricity, but do not be deterred: that "brownish curiosity" has been the historic dessert fruit of choice of countless connoisseurs, John Parkinson speaking in 1627 "of the pleasant sweetness of the fruit when mellow," and the illustrious British oenophile George Saintsbury, in his *Notes on a Cellar* of 1920, declaring the medlar "an admirable and distinguished thing . . ." and "the one fruit which seems to me to go best with all wine . . ."As medlars are not broadly carried, most any cultivar you chance upon will be of interest, although the British pomologist Robert Hogg observed in 1862 that the English heirloom 'Nottingham' was "the best medlar in cultivation" and the "more highly flavored." Also noteworthy, however, are the varieties 'Monstrous,' with notably large fruit, and 'Old Dutch,' an antique cultivar originating in Holland.

The medlar is a diminutive tree of uncommon beauty, with large, luxuriantly green leaves turning an opulent crimson in fall, and accompanied by masses of large, white, 5-petaled flowers in May, all held on sharp-angled branches, which create a true "crown" effect habitwise to about 20 feet. As the medlar is happily self-fertile, long-lived, uncomplainingly soil adaptable and pest-free, and hardy to at least USDA zone 5, do yourself a favor: search out this entirely exceptional food plant. Pick fruit on a dry sunny day after the first heavy frost, and allow to "blett" in a cool, dry space until skin turns deep brown and they have reached their soft edibility. In deference to this anciently favored fruit's being likened to a "richly spiced applesauce or baked apple," how about a medlar tart recipe of 1653: "Take Medlers that be rotten, and stamp them, and set them upon a chafin-dish with coales, and beat two yolks of Eggs, boyling till it be somewhat thick, then season it with Sugar, Cinamon, and Ginger, and lay it in paste."

ॐ

46. Mulberry 'Dwarf Weeping Black'
Morus nigra

"Here we go round the mulberry bush,
On a cold and frosty morning."

—English nursery rhyme, eighteenth century

Fascinatingly, this familiar nursery rhyme was first sung by the inmates of the Wakefield House of Correction in England as they exercised around a mulberry tree in the prison grounds, and originated from some moment between 1786 and 1800. There are three basic types of mulberry: the white mulberry, *Morus alba*, native to China; the black mulberry, *Morus nigra*, anciently native to Iran and Mesopotamia; and the red mulberry, *Morus rubra*, native to the eastern United States, all being extremely antique to their natural habitats. The white mulberry, of course, is famous for its relationship with the discovery and manufacture of silk, in China, legend holding that it was the empress Si Ling Chi who discovered silk 5,000 years ago when, while sipping tea in the palace garden, a cocoon fell into her cup from a white mulberry and, as she watched, a slim white thread unraveled itself.

There are multiple references to the black mulberry in the Bible, 2 Samuel 5:24 reporting aggressively: "And let it be, when thou hearest the sound of a going in the tops of the mulberry trees, that then thou shalt bestir thyself: for then shall the LORD go out before thee, to smite the host of the Philistines." We also find mention of the mulberry in Ovid's telling of the sad tale of Pyramus and Thisbe, who, Romeo and Juliet-like, suicided in a mulberry's shade, the fruit, famously, being turned from white to black by their blood. The black mulberry was probably introduced into northern Europe and England by the Romans, and there are a host of famously ancient black mulberries in Great Britain, one at Syon House in Brentford said to be the oldest in England and introduced from Persia in 1548.

Mulberry 'Dwarf Weeping Black'

While northern Native American prehistory is a fairly sketchy chunk of time, certainly the red mulberry has grown in North America for thousands of years, the Cherokee Nation using an infusion of its bark to treat worms, dysentery, and as a purgative and laxative, and the Creeks employing an infusion of the root for both "weakness" and urinary tract infections. As well, the Cherokees, Comanches, Seminoles, and Choctaws all consumed red mulberries whole, juiced, dried, and baked, and wove cloaks and made baskets from their fibrous inner bark and young shoots. Our common red mulberry is a handsome tree, growing from 30 to 70 feet, forming a dense head of branches typically wider than high, and often sporting variously lobed leaves.

However, here I advise you to turn your attention to one of the Eurasian types, the unique 'Dwarf Weeping Black' mulberry. First of all, the black mulberry has always boasted the sweetest, juiciest fruit of the tribe. Secondly, although most black mulberries are also the tenderest of the clan, the 'Dwarf Weeping Black' mulberry is far tougher, being dramatically hardy to USDA zones 3 to 9. Additionally, it is happily self-fertile, the perfect size for any garden at only 12 feet tall and wide, with a notably graceful weeping habit that can trail to the ground, and handsome green, slightly serrated leaves. Mulberries themselves mainly resemble a large blackberry and can be so tasty, the great American reformer Henry Ward Beecher stated in 1846: "I had rather have one tree of . . . Mulberries than a bed of strawberries." Therefore, do plant one and, from these luscious berries, why not concoct a rich mulberry sauce to accompany a duck or chicken? To 2 cups crushed mulberries, add $1/2$ cup of brown sugar and a teaspoon each of cloves and allspice, bring to a boil, simmer until thick, stirring often, sieve to remove seeds, and serve.

47. Nectarine 'Mericrest'

Prunus persica var. *nectarina*

"The nectarine and curious peach
into my hands themselves do reach . . ."

—Andrew Marvell, "The Garden," 1681

First, let us clear up the nagging debate concerning the parentage of the nectarine. Contrary to popular opinion, the nectarine is not the wayward spawn of those promiscuous *Prunus* cousins the peach and the plum, but is simply a fuzzless peach, spontaneously mutated in China, most probably around the first century B.C. Oddly, spontaneous mutation appears to be this fruit's most unique and enduring trait, as peach seeds may grow into nectarine trees, and vice versa, no less an authority than Charles Darwin having this to say in his *Variation of Animals and Plants Under Domestication* of 1868: "We have excellent evidence of peach-stones producing nectarine-trees, and of nectarine-stones producing peach-trees, of the same tree bearing peaches and nectarines . . . as well as fruit in part nectarine and in part peach . . ." I call it shameless. Apparently for good reason, in their most antique stage, there was absolutely no differentiation between the profligate pair, the eminent American pomologist U. P. Hedrick declaring in his *The Peaches of New York* of 1917: "The established history of the nectarine goes back 2,000 years and then merges into that of the peach."

The esteemed nineteenth-century French botanist Alphonse de Candolle reported that he "sought in vain for a proof that the nectarine existed in Italy in the time of ancient Rome," and it is Jacques Daléchamps, the French botanist, who finally gives the first reliable description of the nectarine in his *Historia generalis plantarum* of 1587, calling it *nucipersica* or "Persian nut" because of its purported resemblance to the walnut. The word *nectarine*, clearly derivative of "nectar," seems to have been first coined by John Parkinson in his *Paradisi in Sole Paradisus Terrestris* of 1629, calling it ". . . more firme than the peach and

NECTARINE 'MERICREST'

more delectable in taste, and is therefore of more esteem, and that worthily." We find the first mention of the nectarine in America in historian Robert Beverly's *The History and Present State of Virginia* of 1722, although some feel they must have been delivered into California by the Spanish at a far earlier date.

Nectarines fall into two basic categories, yellow and white-fleshed, and, as the yellow types are more healthful, here I will urge you toward the 'Mericrest' nectarine, a yellow-fleshed type first bred by Professor E. M. Meader of the New Hampshire Experimental Station in the middle of the last century from the 'Nectarest' and 'Merideth' varieties. Among its virtues are extreme cold and frost hardiness, braving even subzero temperatures like a trooper (USDA zone 5 to 8), and both a "freestone" and self-fruitful habit. The 'Mericrest,' like all nectarines and peaches, is also a delightfully decorative tree, and will grace your garden with a bounty of frilly pink blossom in spring, and lavish yields of large, red-skinned, yellow-fleshed fruit with an intensely rich, tangy flavor in late summer or fall. Additionally, the 'Mericrest' has recently been made available on subzero dwarfing stock, this especially hardy tree achieving the ultimate height of only 8 to 10 feet, which is the perfect size for any yard.

The 'Mericrest,' like all members of the *Prunus* clan, will crave full sun, a well-drained position, and enjoy being pruned to an open center for optimal sunlight exposure and yield. As well, nectarines are prone to the pests and pestilences common to soft fruit trees, so some program of pest control will be not go unrewarded. The 'Mericrest' nectarine is happily low in calories, a fantastic source of vitamin A, and will deliver to you excellent doses of vitamin C, beta-carotene, and potassium, so why not try this sweet idea spooned over vanilla ice cream: cut 4 nectarines in quarters, toss with 1/3 cup marsala wine and 1/2 teaspoon cinnamon, and pan fry in butter until golden?

48. Ollalieberry
49. Youngberry
❦ 50. Marionberry ❦
Rubus ursinus hybrids

"You ate that first one and its flesh was sweet
Like thickened wine: summer's blood was in it
Leaving stains upon the tongue and lust for picking."

—Seamus Heaney, "Blackberry Picking," 1966

I have chosen to lump youngberries, ollalieberries, and marionberries into another bubbling pot of bramble soup as, in point of fact, that's exactly where they belong. All are twentieth-century offspring of the ancient, and, in some precincts, dangerously ubiquitous "bramble" or blackberry, each finding in its parentage some of the antique blackberry's alternatively named modern progeny as well. I am still sorely tempted to say that, no matter what they choose to call themselves, they are all blackberries of some shape and description and the hell with it, but I persevere for your sake, dear reader. All of these, ultimately, are really dewberries as, versus the true blackberry's erect caning posture, these have all inherited the dewberry's more prostrate, crawling habit, although all are generally cultivated in some erect fashion or other on trellises or frames.

We will begin our exploration of these defiant un-blackberries with the youngberry (*Rubus ursinus* v. 'Young'), which was developed in 1905 by one B. M. Young of Morgan City, Louisiana, when he crossed a 'Phenomenal' blackberry (a cultivar very similar to the loganberry) with a 'Mayes' dewberry. Boasting the dewberry's signature prickly, trailing habit, deeply ruby to almost black fruit, and a tart but still winning flavor, the youngberry was coddled and stroked in Mr. Young's backyard for over twenty years, until, in 1926, it was finally introduced for public consumption. Similar in taste and appearance to the boysenberry

MARIONBERRY

YOUNGBERRY

(surprise, surprise), the youngberry quickly overshadowed the problematic loganberry (which, as we have noted, was only fit for fillings and juice when sweetened and too fragile to ship) and soon became the canning and jarring berry of choice in the "big berry" states of California, Oregon, and Washington. It is still widely grown in the northwest.

The ollalieberry, coined from the Pacific Northwest Indian word for "berry," was created in 1935 by Oregon grower George F. Waldo, when he crossed a blackberry, a loganberry, and, naturally, as the *Rubus* family is clearly rife with incestuous activity, a youngberry. The glossy black ollalieberry, slightly longer and more slender than the boysenberry, is noted for its tangy flavor, and, although an Oregon native, is currently widely cultivated in California as it has the advantage of a shorter winter chilling requirement than the boysenberry, making it more adaptable to the relatively balmy California coast. As well, unlike many blackberry varieties, it is completely resistant to the dreaded *verticillium* wilt, an extremely trying soil-borne fungal disease that can infect *Rubus* canes, its resistance being a very happy thing indeed.

Later in the twentieth century, the marionberry, when it wasn't being the cocaine sniffing, prostitute-fondling mayor of Washington, D.C., was traveling on an ascendant path to become perhaps the most popular blackberry descendant in history, mainly due to its famous quality when processed. Also bred by the celebrated George F. Waldo in Marion County, Oregon, in 1956, from the 'Chehalem' blackberry and, naturally, the ollalieberry, and specifically for the climatic considerations of the fertile northwest, the marionberry is considered by many berry aficionados to be the *n'est plus ultra* of berries, yielding an "intensely aromatic bouquet" described by connoisseurs as "akin to an earthy cabernet." Currently considered to be "the pride of Oregon," the marionberry is the worldwide gourmet "blackberry" of choice for canning, freezing, pies, jams, jellies, and ice creams.

In general, dewberry-type blackberries are more tender and prone to frost damage than their erect caning cousins, although, with proper mulching, all three of these should be hardy down to at least USDA zone 6. As all of these are most easily grown on trellises, the cultural key, in late summer or fall after fruiting, is to remove the spent *floricanes* on the trellis, prune to the strongest 6 or 8 *primocanes*, and then coil them onto the ground and mulch heavily. In spring, only when danger of frost is past, the mulched *primocanes*, now second-year *floricanes*, may be unearthed and reattached to your trellising. Later in the season, near blooming, a spritz of foliar fertilizer like nitrogen sulfate will give your plants a goose before fruiting and help produce the sweetest berries.

All of these would also be an excellent choice for the concoction of a rich berry chutney. Combine 2 pints picked-over berries in a saucepan with 1 cup each chopped onion, balsamic vinegar, and brown sugar, half a cup of fresh, chopped ginger, and 2 chopped garlic cloves, along with a sachet of 6 peppercorns and a tablespoon of pickling spice. Bring to a boil, reduce to a simmer, and cook until the onions are soft and clear. Remove sachet, cool mixture, throw in a handful of chopped mint, and serve to accompany a roast bit of game or such.

OLLALIEBERRY

Orange 'Moro'

51. Orange 'Moro'
❧ 52. Orange 'Washington Navel' ❧
Citrus sinensis

"Eating an orange
While making love
Makes for bizarre enj-
oyment thereof."

—Tom Lehrer, American humorist, b. 1928

DNA evidence suggests the sweet orange (*Citrus sinensis*), versus its bosom companion the sour orange (*Citrus aurantium*), which has a bit of citron (*Citrus medica*) in its parentage, is a spawn of the pummelo (*Citrus grandis*) and the mandarin (*Citrus reticulata*). Augustin Pyramus de Candolle maintained in the nineteenth century that the Burmese peninsula and southern China were their original homes, and oranges were certainly known in the Indo-Orient as long ago as 3000 B.C. It is interesting to note that, while classical botanists from Theophrastus right through Pliny make liberal mention of the citron, there is not a single mention of the orange. It is believed an orange of some sort was delivered into the Mediterranean by the Moors sometime before the ninth century A.D., and it is known that the warrior chieftain Al-Mansur, Muslim caliph of Andalusia, grew them in Cordoba, Spain, by 976 A.D. Marco Polo saw oranges under cultivation near the straits of Hormuz in Iran in the thirteenth century, and identified them as "apples of paradise," which certainly must have added fuel to that always exciting "golden apple" debate.

The first definitive European reference to a *Citrus sinensis* seems to appear in the fifteenth century, although, generally commingled with its less tasty relation the *Citrus aurantium*, it seems to have languished for a bit until people finally noticed that there were two distinct varieties, and that the sweet type was clearly an edible acquaintance worth cultivating.

In 1499, it is recorded that Louis XII was given a sweet orange tree as a wedding present by the Spanish queen Leonora of Castille, and it was reportedly Sir Francis Carew of Beddington in Surrey who, in the late sixteenth century, introduced the first sweet oranges into England, the plants apparently purchased during a 1562 visit to Paris. He planted them directly into his garden and famously over-wintered them in portable heated sheds to the apparent delight of all of Elizabethan England, John Evelyn recounting in 1700 that "the oranges were planted in the open ground & secured in winter only by a Tabernacle of boards, & stoves, removable in summer."

By the mid-seventeenth century, Europe had been swept by what can only be described as "sweet orange mania," and no royal parterre was complete without a lane flanked with potted specimens through which one could stroll to admire the gregarious fruit and glossy foliage and inhale the honeyed scent of the incomparable white blossoms. Orangeries were soon all the rage, John Parkinson reporting in 1629: "some keepe them in great square boxes and lift them to and fro by iron hooks on the sides, or cause them to be rowled by trundles, or small wheeles under them to place them in a house or close gallerie for the winter time." Perhaps the most famous European orangerie was built by Louis XIV between 1684 and 1686 at Versailles, measuring an extraordinary 509 feet in length. Meanwhile, in southern Europe, where the climate was more accommodating, the Bourbon and Spanish monarchs began the planting of vast groves of *Citrus sinensis* in suitable regions of Spain, Portugal, and Italy.

Christopher Columbus delivered the orange to Hispaniola (Haiti) on his second voyage in 1493 and Ponce de León carried it into Florida in 1521, but there is no evidence that either was a "sweet" type. A large number of taxonomists believe the *Citrus sinensis* did not enter North America until 1769, when it was introduced from Mexico to California's first Franciscan mission at San Diego by Padre Junipero Serra. In any case, the sweet orange arrived upon our shores, established itself in several winning climates, and the two types we will glow about here I think, as they say at the dog show, are the "best in class" of those currently available. If you can grow one in your yard or, better yet, a pair

Orange 'Washington Navel'

in big Versailles boxes flanking a door or gateway, I salute you for both your intelligence and taste.

Therefore, an episodic tale: in 1820, a single mutation in a grove of *Citrus sinensis* planted at a monastery in Bahia Blanca, Brazil, sported a belly button. In 1870, a few grafted trees were sent as diplomatic favors from Bahia Blanca to Washington, D.C., to be distributed to more favorable United States–growing locations. In 1873, Eliza Tibbet of Riverside, California, received 3 grafted seedlings of this sweet orange with the appealing deformity, and, by 1878, she had three fruit-bearing trees. Today, we are all eating the descendants of the 'Washington Navel' (also known as the 'Bahia' and 'Riverside' navel for its multiple homes), it being most notable for the tiny "twin" fruit embedded in the rind opposite its stem, looking for all the world like a human navel. Widely recognized as the orange gold standard for its large, nearly seedless, sweet, juicy, easy-to-peel fruit, the 'Washington Navel' is undoubtedly the variety you lunge for at your local supermarket.

Although ancient sites in India, China, and Vietnam are mentioned, until very recently, most botanists believed that the "blood" ("Maltese") orange originated on the island of Malta in the Mediterranean, thus "Maltese." Scattered claques still support these claims, most particularly the Maltese, where the heraldic emblem of the town of Lija displays three oranges rampant and the motto *Suavi Fructo Rubeo*: "With Sweet Fruits I Redden." There is some evidence that a ruby-fleshed (thus "blood") orange existed in China by the fifteenth century A.D., and the first European depiction of a blood orange seems to occur in the Jesuit botanist Giovanni Battista Ferrari's *Hesperides sive de Malorum Aureorum cultura* of 1646, which further maintained that it was delivered into Italy from the Philippines by a Genovese missionary. Whatever the truth, there are now three basic types: the Italian 'Tarocco,' the Spanish 'Sanguinello,' and the 'Moro,' a more recent hybrid out of San Diego, and the one I will recommend here. The medium-sized 'Moro' is the most reliably colorful of the clan, with deep ruby flesh and a thin, red-blushed rind (parenthetically, because of the blood orange's richly crimson interior coloration, it is the only member of the *Citrus* clan to be a healthy source of free radical–fighting anthocyanins as well as the more expected vitamin C). Additionally, it may be kept to 6 to 8 feet with judicious pruning.

Gloriously beautiful, self-fertile, and hardy to USDA zone 9, both the 'Washington Navel' and the 'Moro' will reward you with a handsome small habit, glossy green foliage, heavenly scented, 5-petaled white blossoms, and exceptional fruit. And, by the way, an orange of any sunny hue is one of the few fruit plants that will achieve blossom and both ripe and unripe fruit all at once, for a truly show-stopping display. John Parkinson comments in his *Paradisi in Sole Paradisus Terrestris* of 1629 that "orenges are used as a sawce for many sortes of meats, in respect of their sweete sowernesse, giving a rellish of delight, whereinsoever they are used," so why not a zesty, roasted fowl *a l'orange* this very night?

❦ 53. Pawpaw 'Sunflower' ❦
Asimina triloba

"Pickin' up pawpaws, put 'em in your pockets,
Way down yonder in the pawpaw patch."

—Traditional American folk song, nineteenth century

Indigenous to North America, ranging from Florida to southern Ontario, and bearing North America's largest edible native fruit, it is fascinating to me that this hardy, indigenous food plant is almost totally unknown as an edible today. Prehistoric remains confirm the pawpaw's incredible antiquity, "pawpaw" most likely deriving from the Spanish *papaya*, as both plants share the traits of edible fruit and large, tropical-looking leaves. The earliest mention of the pawpaw dates to Hernanado de Soto's 1540 expedition to the lower Mississippi, where he noted Native American pawpaw cultivation. Pawpaws were a food staple for many Native American tribes, who called them *arawak*, and it is not unusual for clumps of pawpaws to mark the locations of former Native American villages.

In 1736, America's first great botanist, John Bartram, sent pawpaw specimens to England, and chilled pawpaw was apparently a favored dessert of George Washington's. In 1810, Meriwether Lewis and William Clark, journeying through western Missouri, reported, "our party entirely out of provisions, subsisting on poppaws . . . ," and, in 1905, pawpaw breeder James A. Little, in his succinctly named treatise *The Pawpaw*, stated: "We can never realize what a great blessing the pawpaw was to the first settlers . . . The pawpaw and a few other wild fruits . . . were all their dependence so far as fruit was concerned . . ." During the Great Depression, the pawpaw famously supplemented destitute diets with healthy and free fruit, ultimately acquiring the slang sobriquets "Indiana banana," "Michigan banana," and "Kentucky banana," depending on where it was being consumed.

Then, somehow, after World War II, with the advent of imported

Pawpaw 'Sunflower'

fruit types, interest in pawpaws waned almost to nonexistence. To be frank, the large, tropically beautiful leaves and the sizeable maroon blossoms of the pawpaw, while certainly striking, are both, shall we say, of a "controversial" fragrance, some calling the leaves "malodorous" and others feeling the flowers give off the scent of rotting meat. Even the fruit takes a few olfactory knocks, as noted in this mainly laudatory statement in *The Journal of Heredity* of 1916: "Its creamy pulp is of exquisite texture in the mouth, while its distinctive flavor and aroma, often too pungent, give it a decided individuality . . ." However, for a once popular, hardy, and near nationally available fruit to go entirely underground just for the sake of its questionable scent seems harsh.

Still, the pawpaw does have its champions: the Blandy Experimental Farm, home of the Virginia State Arboretum, has been collecting pawpaws since 1926, and, in 1988, Neal Peterson of West Virginia founded the Pawpaw Foundation, which oversees two orchards totaling over 1,900 trees at the University of Maryland. The currently available varieties 'Fairchild' and 'Mitchell' are thought to have the best-tasting fruit, but will need cross-pollinators, so it is to the self-fruitful 'Sunflower' I will turn your attention now. Hardy to at least USDA zone 5, 'Sunflower' will grow to about 15 to 25 feet, with those arresting if divisive tropical leaves and blossoms, and pendulous clusters of light green fruit turning yellowish when ripe and weighing from 8 to 12 ounces.

Each 'Sunflower' fruit will reward you with 3 times as much vitamin C, 6 times as much riboflavin, 3 times as much potassium, and 14 times as much niacin as an apple, and more phosphorus, magnesium, iron, zinc, copper, and manganese than an apple, banana, or orange. Tasting like a delicious blend of banana and vanilla custard, pawpaws can be substituted for bananas in most any recipe, so let me suggest here a pawpaw pie for your "patch": combine 1 1/2 cups pawpaws (peeled and seeded) with an egg, a cup each of sugar and milk, and 1/4 teaspoon salt in a pot, stir over medium heat until thickened, pour into a baked pie shell, and chill.

ॐ

54. Peach 'Belle of Georgia'
55. Peach 'Indian Blood'
Prunus persica

In the Taoist religion, the peach is honored both as a symbol of femi-
nine sexuality and of human longevity. The mythical "old man,"
Shou Lu, is often portrayed with his finger stuck into the suggestive
suture of this fuzzy fruit. Make of this what you will.

China is the antique birthplace of the peach, where they were considered the most sacred plant of the Taoist religion as far back as
the tenth century B.C., *Tao* actually translating to "peach."
Despite its fuzzy familiarity, the peach is somewhat of a botanical mystery,
being one of the few edible food plants that has never been identified in a
truly wild state, indicating incredibly ancient culture in China. In
Chinese legend, the peach grew in the goddess Hsi Wang Mu's garden,
fruiting only once every 3,000 years and conferring eternal life on those
who were lucky enough to merit a bite. Selection and cultivation of the
peach began in China as early as 2000 B.C.; by 300 B.C. it had been
imported first into Persia, and then into Greece, and by the first century
A.D. it was under extensive cultivation in the Roman Empire. The peach
was given its misguided *persica* designation in 370 B.C. by none other than
Theophrastus, Greek father of botany, who erroneously believed that
Persia was its country of origin. The peach made its way into England
and France in the late sixteenth century, and was first introduced into
the New World in 1562 by French explorers near Mobile, Alabama.

Native Americans, who were great peach aficionados, are credited
with moving the peach west across the United States with their seasonal
migrations, and interestingly, in part because fairly any peach pit when
planted will result in a tree, the early peach trees imported into the New
World grew with such carefree abandon that post-sixteenth-century
settlers supposed them to be native to the Americas, William Penn
recording in 1683 that dense native thickets of wild peach trees were full

PEACH 'BELLE OF GEORGIA'

of fruit just north of Philadelphia. Sadly, through over-hybridization by the commercial peach industry to improve hardiness and storability, modern peach trees seem to have lost that astounding vigor that described their earliest American habits, and most commonly available trees now have a life span of only 8 to 10 years.

As with all ancient edible plants, the peach figured in a variety of medicinal employments, Nicholas Culpeper echoing the ancient Chinese view and reporting in his *Herball* of 1653 that "Venus owns this tree" and that "the fruit promotes lust." He also informs us that "nothing is better to purge choler and jaundice . . ." and that "if the kernels be bruised and boiled in vinegar . . . and applied to the head, it marvellously makes the hair to grow again upon bald places . . ." Modern medicine tells us that peaches are powerhouses of beta-carotene and vitamin A, excellent sources of vitamins B and C, and are valued for their diuretic, digestive, and laxative properties. One is compelled to mention here that peach leaves, flowers, bark, and especially the pits contain cyanogenic glycosides, which produce cyanide, so, whatever Culpeper may recommend, ingestion of any of the above in quantity is distinctly unadvisable.

In general, peaches fall into three categories, depending on how firmly the flesh of the peach "clings" to the pit. "Clingstones" are so named because their flesh grips like a long-lost lover. And although their flesh is usually juicier and sweeter than the other types, it is also softer and more bruisable, making them difficult to transport and store with any success: this the peach you commonly find canned in syrup. "Freestones," as you might expect, possess firmer, less juicy flesh that detaches easily from the stone, making them an excellent choice for fresh eating: this is the type you customarily find in your grocery store. "Semi-freestones" are a modern hybrid of the two other types, combining their best attributes.

Culturally, I will admit outright that peaches are not the easiest of fruit plants, so I believe the best I can do here is to select two classic cultivars that are as docile and uncomplaining as possible. The beautiful and productive nineteenth-century American variety 'Belle of Georgia' is one of the first great natively bred peaches, developed in about 1880 along with the equally illustrious 'Elberta' peach. An authentic

American beauty, white of flesh, blushing of skin, and infinitely sweet to the taste, 'Belle of Georgia' will reward you with gorgeous red flowers in spring, a "freestone" habit, admirable disease resistance, longevity and bud hardiness, and excellent adaptation to USDA zones 5 to 8, as well as availability on both dwarf and nondwarf rootstock. The entrancing 'Belle of Georgia' is longer lived than most, but as mentioned, peaches are not trees with which one will grow old. That said, the 'Belle of Georgia' is amazingly precocious and will usually bear fruit in the second year after planting.

The 'Indian Blood' is an antique "clingstone" variety believed to be descended from the ancient French variety *Sanguinole* ("bloody"), and imported by the Spanish into Mexico in the sixteenth century. This heavenly peach, tiger-striped red and yellow with sweet crimson flesh, was planted throughout the American South, but most especially in Georgia, by the Cherokee Indians and, by 1810, Thomas Jefferson had planted 41 stones of the "Black Plumb Peach of Georgia" at Monticello and had become so enamored of it that he created a hedge of over 1,000 trees around his gardens. Ultimately, the "Black Peach of Georgia" became known as the 'Indian Blood,' uniting the "blood" of the French *Sanguinole* parent to the "native" variety so beloved by the Cherokees. Here I will admit to a further bit of mystery concerning this peach as, of the many sources with which I have conferred, some laud its relatively diminutive size, while others state that it can achieve an astounding 12 inches in girth. Photographs seem to bear out both theories, even on the same plant. Whatever its ultimate stature, however, all sources seem to agree that, culinarily, the ruby-fleshed 'Indian Blood' is one of the most delicious peaches in existence, and, culturally, one of the easiest and most productive to grow, being self-fertile and hardy in USDA zones 5 to 8, and only requiring 700 to 800 hours of annual chilling in order to bear fruit.

Like all peach trees, both 'Belle of Georgia' and 'Indian Blood' will enjoy being pruned to an open center when young, and the fruit thinned to 1 peach to every 6 inches of limb after annual blooming for optimal development. And, as with all orchard trees, a dormant oil spray will be helpful before blossoming, as will a dose of fungicide and insecticide as your tree begins to develop fruit. Does this all sound like way too much

PEACH 'INDIAN BLOOD'

chemistry and effort? To be honest, it is right on the cusp. But to pluck a warm 'Belle of Georgia' or 'Indian Blood' off your own tree and sink your teeth into its honeyed creamy or crimson flesh? Well, I believe old Count Dracula was onto something. Serve fresh peaches to your guests sliced atop a scoop or two of vanilla ice cream. Perfection.

❧ 56. Pear 'Doyenne du Comice' ❧
57. Pear 'Shenandoah'

Pyrus communis

"The pear must be approached, as its feminine nature indicates, with discretion and reverence; it withholds its secrets from the merely hungry."

—Edward Bunyard, *The Anatomy of Dessert*, 1929

The genus *Pyrus*, encompassing about 22 separate species, is another absurdly ancient member of the greater rose (*Rosaceae*) family. Thought to be originally native to the northern Middle East, the wild pear, like many ancient food plants, was a small, bitter, barely edible thing. However, culture of this antique food plant came very early on, and, as long ago as 5000 B.C., the Chinese diplomat Feng Li had famously given up his civil career to devote himself to the grafting of pears and other fruits. It is known from carbon-dated seed remains that, by 3500 B.C., the ancient lake dwellers of Switzerland were dallying with the pear. Oddly, *Pyrus communis*, the European pear and antique antecedent of most modern varieties, is a species that does not occur in nature and is thought by most botanists to be a spontaneous offspring of *Pyrus caucasia*, the wild or thorny pear, and *Pyrus nivalis*, the snow pear. By the first century A.D., *Pyrus communis* cultivars had been divided by Pliny the Elder into two groups: the "proud" pears, so called because they fruited early and would not be "kept," and the "winter" or late pears, which fruited in the fall and were generally used for cooking.

Cato the Elder recorded 6 varieties in his *De Agri Cultura* of 150 B.C., Pliny a total of 41 in his *Natural History* of 77 A.D., and Palladius 56 in his *De Re Rustica* in the fourth century A.D. By the early seventeenth century, Cosimo de Medici II, grand duke of Tuscany, was offering his guests an astonishing 209 different types of pears, and by the end of it, under Louis XIV, the French were growing over 300 different varieties.

PEAR 'DOYENNE DU COMICE'

The pear was introduced into England by the conquering Romans in about 55 B.C., and by 1653, Nicholas Culpeper was commenting in his *Herbal* that "Pear Trees are so well known, that they need no description," also noting on a helpful medical note that "The wild Pears do sooner close up the lips of green wounds than others." By 1842, more than 700 European pear types were documented by the Royal Horticultural Society in Great Britain. The Belgian monk Nicolas Hardenpont is credited with producing the first pear with the honeyed "buttery" flesh that identifies the best European pears in the early eighteenth century. The cultural mantle was then inherited by Jean Baptiste van Mons, a Belgian physician, who bred no less than 40 different "beurre" types between 1800 and 1842.

Pear seeds were first received into Massachusetts Bay on March 16, 1629, and, in 1630, the first American pear seedling was delivered to Governor John Endicott in Salem, Massachusetts, by the English ship *Arabella*. The 'Endicott' pear still stands in Danversport, Massachusetts, having survived transplantation, multiple hurricanes, and vandalism, at an astounding 376 years of age. French missionaries carried the pear to the banks of the Detroit River by 1705, and, by 1771, the Robert Prince Nursery of Flushing, New York, listed an impressive 42 varieties. The New World emphatically embraced the ambrosial fruit of the pear until unforeseen disaster struck in the guise of *Erwinia amylovora*, a bacteria native to American woodlands and commonly known as fireblight, which would not just weaken or maim the pear, but kill the tree outright. And worse, there is still no known cure, and the occurrence of fireblight was and still is completely erratic, decades passing without incidence followed by weeks of abrupt annihilation. Therefore, enter the *Pyrus communis*'s Far Eastern cousin, *P. serotina* (*P. pyrifolia*), imported into North America early in the nineteenth century and commonly called the "Sand pear" for its gritty, less than appealing flesh, but possessed of one dazzling attribute: fireblight resistance.

Subsequent breeding of the "Sand pear" with its European cousins has produced a swarm of good-tasting, disease-resistant cultivars, and the just-off-the-line 'Shenandoah' is the currently touted *pièce de résistance*, with seemingly excellent everything. The original seedling of

'Shenandoah' was selected in 1985 by horticulturist Richard Bell at the USDA Appalachian Fruit Research Station in Kearneysville, West Virginia, from a cross of 'Max Red Bartlett' with the beguilingly named "US 56112-146." This luscious new cultivar's fruit is an agreeable yellow/green flushed with red at maturity, and its higher-than-average acidity, balanced with an equally high sucrose level, gives it a marvelously rich, juicy and buttery, sweet/tart flavor. Additionally, 'Shenandoah' is notably precocious, with first fruit setting about 2 years after planting, and with none of the biennial fruiting habit common to other cultivars.

Although that blessed host of fireblight-resistant hybrids has, thankfully, reintroduced pear culture to the southern and eastern United States, I would be remiss if I did not recommend to those of you who can grow her the historical and still reigning queen of pear culture, the incomparable 'Doyenne du Comice.' Translating literally to "grandest lady of the show," the 'Doyenne du Comice' was first introduced to society at the *Comice Horticole* in Angers, France, in 1849. Content to shroud her luminosity beneath a demure plain-Janeness, this grand lady's "broad, blunt, large and somewhat dumpy" shape and yellow/green complexion freckled and mottled with russeting are emphatically unremarkable. However, one has only to sink one's teeth into a perfectly mature 'Doyenne' to encounter what has been heralded by pomologists and gastronomes alike as the finest "beurre" pear in existence, twentieth-century American food writer Waverly Root, among countless others, extolling her "sweetly and subtly perfumed," meltingly buttery flesh, and Britain's Royal Horticultural Society awarding her its coveted Garden Merit Award in 1993.

That said, allow me to verge on the brusque: culturally, pears can be perfectly exasperating. They are prone to a variety of blights and diseases, and, while 'Shenandoah' is fireblight resistant, 'Doyenne du Comice' and many others are not, and no European pears are self-fruitful. Additionally, 'Doyenne du Comice' may also be a bit slow to bear, sometimes requiring as long as 8 to 10 years unless grafted onto dwarf quince stock, and pears can also be exceedingly finicky about their time of harvest: too soon and they can be tasteless and coarse-fleshed, too late and they are little better than brown mush when they reach the

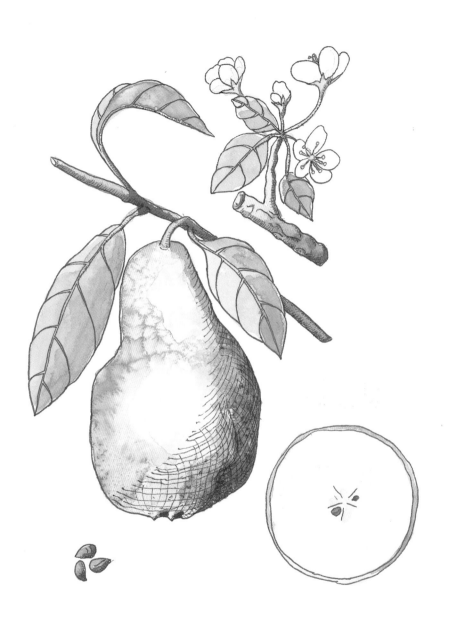

Pear 'Shenandoah'

table. As the great nineteenth-century transcendentalist philosopher Ralph Waldo Emerson so perceptively put it: "There are only ten minutes in the life of a pear when it is perfect to eat."

Still, for a chance to sample either of these uniquely ambrosial cultivars at that perfect moment, and to enjoy that beautiful flurry of white blossoms in spring, why not plant one of each with one or two other pear varieties for cross-pollination as Louis XIV did at Versailles, trained in a double or triple row on espalier wires as a fencelike feature in your garden, and hope for the best? If the best arrives, sink your teeth into it posthaste or, better yet, I can't think of a more appealing candidate for a grunt or crumble.

❧ 58. Persimmon 'Jiro' ❧
Diospyros kaki

There is a saying in the American southeast, where persimmons grow
wild, that they are only "good for dogs, hogs, and 'possums."

Members of the greater ebony (*Ebenaceae*) family, persimmons
come in there two prominent types, the tiny American persimmon (*Diospyros virginiana*) and the larger, more familiar
Oriental or Japanese persimmon (*Diospyros kaki*). The Latin *Diospyros*
optimistically translates to "grain of Jove," but the persimmon's potentially over-astringent personality has been an issue across both its early
cultures. The grape-sized, mouth-puckering American persimmon is an
antique denizen of neglected pastures and fence rows throughout
Maryland, Virginia, and the Carolinas. The larger, more familiar Oriental
(Japanese or *kaki*) persimmon, despite being originally native to China, is
universally identified with Japan and numbers about 2,000 different cultivars. It is further divided into two other über-camps, the brilliantly
orange, acorn-shaped, highly astringent 'Hachiya,' which dominates the
commercial market and, like the American persimmon, is only remotely
edible when soft and fully ripe, and the 'Fuyu' type, also bright orange but
squatter, famously nonastringent, and eaten crisp like an apple.

Captain John Smith, who founded the first permanent English settle-
ment in America at Jamestown, Virginia, in 1607, said of the American
persimmon: "If it be not ripe it will drawe a mans mouth awrie with
much torment," but further added, "but when it is ripe, it is as delicious
as an Apricock." The key here, clearly, is "when it is ripe," as the tannin
present in a mouthful of unripe American persimmon could probably
remove paint from a car. Called *pasiminan* or *pessamin* by both the
Algonquin Indians who greeted the Jamestown settlers and the Lenapes
with whom William Penn traded, history also records that, during the
Civil War, American persimmon seeds were boiled by soldiers of the
Confederacy into a coffeelike beverage.

PERSIMMON 'JIRO'

It was Commodore Matthew Perry who, after bullying his way into Nagasaki harbor and opening Japan to the West in 1854, returned to the United States with *Diospyros kaki* persimmon trees, completely transforming our notion of what a persimmon could be, and it is to one of these that I will ultimately direct you. However, *en route*, let me stop to laud the American persimmon variety 'Ruby' for its atypically large fruit, exceptional ornamentality, self-fertility, and fine hardiness to USDA zones 5 to 8. That said, if what you covet is that signature orange-lacquered fruit so dear to autumnal tables, an Oriental persimmon is the only way to go, and for ease of both culture and consumption, I am happy to point you toward the 'Fuyu' cultivar 'Jiro.' Also known as the "Apple persimmon," the 'Jiro' is glossily tangerine-hued, medium-sized, flat, and squat. Like all 'Fuyu' persimmons, the 'Jiro' is consumed apple crisp.

'Jiro' has been a traditional commercial favorite for its uncomplaining cheerfulness, lovely habit, and gorgeously healthful fruit. Each firm, crunchy 'Jiro' contains about 118 calories with 31 grams of carbohydrates, and pleasing doses of vitamins A and C, potassium, and beta-carotene, plus a smattering of trace B vitamins. Culturally, 'Jiro' is a very attractive tree growing to about 15 feet high with leathery, dark green, ovate leaves, the leaves turning intensely gregarious shades of yellow, orange, and red under the right autumnal conditions. Female flowers are dainty single ivory blooms with a green calyx, while males are pretty pink-tinged blossoms borne in threes, and 'Jiro' is also conveniently self-fertile, essentially pest- and soil issue–free, and hardy to USDA zones 7 to 10. As noted, 'Jiro' persimmons are as crunchy and sweet as apples and are commonly enjoyed in the Orient peeled and simply sliced, just as one would an apple, which is what I will recommend to you here. Do, however, allow them to languish a while in a silver bowl on a highly polished wooden surface to give you a bit of a visual feast first.

59. Pineapple 'Smooth Cayenne'

Ananas comosus

Love is like
a pineapple,
sweet and
undefinable.

—Piet Hein, "What Love is Like," 2002

The pineapple, a member of the *Bromeliad* family, is an ancient American food plant native to southern Brazil and Paraguay. Domesticated in Pre-Columbian times in the Orinoco and Amazon River basins, it was probably the sea-venturing Guaraní Indians who dispersed the plants from their native Paraguay throughout South and Central America and the West Indies. In an odd duality of sentiment, it is known that early West Indians planted hedges of prickly pineapples around their villages to keep out intruders, while, at the same time, hanging them at their gates to signify welcome and abundance. This latter connotation was adopted by the fifteenth-century Spanish explorers, who carried it back to the Old World, and the pineapple, originally *a-nana*, Caribbean for "fruit" and "excellent," has forever after been symbolic of the twin qualities of bounty and hospitality.

It is Christopher Columbus who is responsible for both the pineapple's current appellation, calling the exotic fruit *piña* because it looked like a pinecone, and its introduction into Europe in 1493. Pineapples remained a rarity destined only for aristocratic tables until 1686, when a Dutch grower, M. Le Cour, successfully cultured the first European pineapples under glass. By the 1690s, all of Europe was lauding them as the horticultural *n'est plus ultra*, and pineapples became so important a symbol of affluence and welcome in the early American colonies that hospitable households would rent one for a day, and then return it to the grocer to be sold to someone who could actually afford to consume it. The pineap-

PINEAPPLE 'SMOOTH CAYENNE'

ple we know today first appeared at the turn of the eighteenth century, after improvement by the ever-industrious Dutch. By 1835, there were 52 varieties listed in Europe, and, by 1856, 70.

As *Bromeliads*, pineapples are spiky, sword-leaved plants from which a single stem and fruit rises centrally, although the pineapple is technically not a single fruit at all, but a "sorosis": a cluster of tiny flowers growing on the plant's spike, each flower ultimately engorging with pulp to form the flesh and one of the meaty "scales" of the pineapple's exterior. Pineapples are an excellent source of manganese and vitamins C and B1, as well as of bromelain, an enzyme with a promising future in the treatment of heart attacks, abscesses, and ulcers. There are two main commercial varieties: the painfully serrated 'Red Spanish' and the 'Smooth Cayenne,' with both a larger and more elongated shape, sweet, deep yellow flesh, and leaves with a smooth, nonthreatening edge, which is why I propose it to you here. First selected and cultivated in Venezuela, the 'Smooth Cayenne' was introduced from Cayenne (French Guiana) into Europe in 1820, eventually reaching the Royal Botanical Gardens at Kew in England, where it was improved and ultimately distributed to Jamaica, Australia, and Hawaii, as it is only truly hardy to USDA zones 10 and 11.

Okay, fine: so most of you can't grow one—only you *can*. The culture of a pineapple top is one of those horticultural diversions familiar to any schoolchild, and, while not a short process, is wildly amusing when it finally pays off. To do so, just cut the top inch of crown off a store-bought 'Smooth Cayenne,' scoop the flesh out of the hollow, and plant shallowly in a pot of well-aerated soil. Keep it moist and warm and in as much sun as is possible, and your 'Smooth Cayenne' will root within weeks, leaf becomingly, flower in about 18 months, and triumphantly fruit about 6 months after that. I believe this is another fantastic salsa idea in the making (lime, cilantro, jalapeño, sweet onion)— perhaps after displaying your pineapple in some place of pride (or renting it briefly to one of your less well-to-do neighbors).

❦ 60. Plum 'Methley' ❦
Prunus salicina

"The branches of the aspen plum
To and fro they sway
How can I not think of her?
But home is far away."

—Confucius, 551–479 B.C.

There are many types of plums but two main families basically own the "fresh edible" category, *Prunus domestica*, which we have investigated through our examination of the greengage, and the one we will explore here, *Prunus salicina*, known as the "Japanese plum," although it is actually native to China. The plum tree plays a significant role in Chinese mythology and is anciently associated with great age, wisdom, and good fortune, and mentions of *Prunus salicina* make frequent appearances in the fifth-century B.C. songs and writings of Confucius. Legend holds that Lao Tse, translating to "The Old Master," purported author of the *Tao Te Ching* and founder of Chinese Taoism in the sixth century B.C., was born under a Japanese plum tree, although other myths maintain that he was bred by a falling star or, alternately, spent 81 years in his mother's womb and finally appeared with a full head of white hair. Your choice. The *Prunus salicina* also figures prominently in *Legends of Three Kingdoms*, the fourteenth-century historical novel by Luó Guànzhong, acclaimed as one of the "Four Classical Novels" of Chinese literature and documenting the turbulent years at the end of the Three Kingdoms period (220–280 A.D.).

Japanese plums were domesticated in Japan by the seventeenth century and introduced into the United States in the late nineteenth, reaching California and grower John Kelsey of Berkeley in 1870. America's most famous breeder of plants, Luther Burbank, picked up the ball in 1885, when he imported 12 plum seeds from Japan, stating that that act

PLUM 'METHLEY'

constituted the "most important importation of fruit bearers ever made at a single time into America." He set about hybridizing literally millions of seedlings with the climatically hardy but far less tasty native American types (*P. americana, P. hortulana, P. munsoniana,* and *P. maritime*), and ultimately developed the antecedents of nearly every current cultivated variety, including the one we will praise here.

The *Prunus salicina* 'Methley,' one of the very few *Prunus salicina* types that is self-fertile, is an extremely pretty, small, spreading tree with a roughish bark, brilliant green foliage, fragrant, 5-petaled, white flowers, and heavy crops of juicy, sweet, red/purple fruit with superb deep crimson flesh. Ripening in June or July, 'Methley' will begin fruiting 2 to 4 years from planting, is tolerant of both heat and short winters, and is hardy in USDA zones 5 through 9. However, although plums are the most tolerant of stone fruits with respect to heavy, wet soils, they are truly happiest in situations where rainfall during the growing season is minimal and humidity is low. 'Methley' will require minimal pruning, best done after flowering when the tree is still leafless, but, like many *Prunus* offspring, will do best when trained to an open center. As well, all plums will benefit from some blossom thinning for optimum fruit production.

'Methley,' like all Japanese plums, is a fantastic source of vitamins C and A, which translates into remarkable antioxidant content, a major force in the battle against heart disease, asthma, colon cancer, and osteo and rheumatoid arthritis. Therefore, why not harvest a few for a classic Chinese plum sauce in honor of this lovely fruit's Oriental heritage? In a saucepan, stir together 1 cup pitted, sliced 'Methley' plums with almost as much sugar, 1/4 cup water, 2 tablespoons vinegar, 1 minced garlic clove, 1 tablespoon each brown sugar and minced onion, and 1 teaspoon each minced ginger and crushed red pepper. Bring to a boil, and then simmer, stirring, till combined and thickened. Serve cooled, wrapped in fresh lettuce leaves with some shredded pork and bean sprouts for a marvelous, light summer meal.

61. Plumcot
62. Pluot
63. Aprium
❧ 64. Peacotum ❧

Prunus armeniaca x *Prunus domestica* (x *Prunus persica*)

The Prunus family is so wantonly profligate, dallying with any sibling, cousin, and even offspring that chances by, it is surprising they aren't illegal in some states.

Welcome to the newest generation of fruit plants. All of these are early-to-late-twentieth-century American hybrids of those ancient and lusty *Prunus* stone fruits—the plum, the apricot, and the peach, which are antiquely native to the Far and Middle East, with the "European" plum (*Prunus domestica*) hailing from Persia, and the apricot (*P. armeniaca*) and peach (*P. persica*) being native to China, although, from their botanical names, you may deduce that these three traveled to Armenia and Persia, respectively, very early on. All of them moved west through trade, were eventually carried into the Mediterranean, mainly with the returning armies of everyone from Alexander the Great in the fourth century B.C. to Julius Caesar in the first, and were, generally, spread northward with the expansion of the Roman Empire, the "European" plums reaching England as early as the eighth century A.D., and peaches and apricots arriving on the northern European scene by the sixteenth century. All three were brought into the New World by the earliest Spanish, Portuguese, or English settlers, where they found welcoming homes in both North and South America.

When I say *Prunus* types are profligate, I do not exaggerate, and the 4 fruits listed in this chapter are weighty evidence of this fact. In fact, I might have listed a total of 10 *Prunus* offspring in this section, but have opted to ignore the "plucot," "nectarcot," "nectaplum," "peachcot," "cherrycot," and "peacherine," at least in the chapter heading, as I

PLUMCOT

PLUOT

APRIUM

PEACOTUM

thought it unfair to give up 6 other really different fruit types for these basic variations on a theme. The first modern *Prunus* hybrid, the "plumcot," was developed by Luther Burbank in 1904, the *Los Angeles Times*, on May 19 of that year, charmingly reporting it as "a result of the happy union between father apricot and mother plum." The plumcot, with its basically equal heritage of plum and apricot, is plumlike in shape with smooth, deep crimson skin; sweet, spicy, red flesh; and, while smelling more of an apricot, has more the flavor of a plum.

After the introduction of the plumcot, it wasn't until the late twentieth century that the *Prunus* hybridizing baton was picked up by Floyd Zaiger of Zaiger's Genetics of Modesto, California, but he gripped it with a vengeance. Founding a genuine family operation in 1971, Floyd, with the aid of his wife Betty Zaiger, daughter Leith Gardner, and sons Gary and Grant Zaiger, are "a family organized to improve fruit worldwide." Over the past 35 years, with a stock of 2,200 plants and through hand pollenization alone, Zaiger's Genetics is pretty much globally unequaled in the development of improved *Prunus* varieties, as well as the plucot, pluot, peacotum, aprium, nectarcot, and nectaplum, and, currently, Zaiger's Genetics holds over 200 U.S. plant patents. Unlike Burbank's plumcot, which was a simple plum x apricot cross, Zaiger's trademarked fruits are the products of years of complex hybridization, requiring several generations of crosses to achieve. Additionally, all of his hybrids are bred to be considerably sweeter than any standard *Prunus*.

The pluot, sometimes marketed as the "dinosaur egg" and being 3/4 plum and 1/4 apricot in parentage, with a dappled, silvery-sheened skin, weighs in more on the plum side; while the plucot, which is basically a plumcot, is felt to savor more of apricot than plum. The aprium, which is 2/3 apricot and 1/3 plum, closely resembles the apricot in shape, flavor, and fuzziness, while the peacotum is a sumptuous amalgam of plum, apricot, and peach, and is thought by fruit aficionados to taste of "fruit punch," although this was apparently not always the case. Robert Woolley of the Dave Wilson Nursery, sole purveyor of Zaiger's plants, remembers initially the taste "was so nasty it would lock your jaw . . ." Clearly, here, Zaiger went back to the horticultural drawing board. Other recent entrants into the *Prunus* fray are the nectarcot, a nectarine/apricot cross, the nectaplum, a nectarine/plum cross, the peachcot, a peach/apricot hybrid, and the cherrycot, a cherry/apricot offspring, each sharing traits of both parents in fairly equal measures and all looking, feeling, and tasting exactly like you would assume.

Can you actually find any of these to plant? The answer is: some. As noted, the Dave Wilson Nursery in Hickman, California, is the sole licensor and primary grower of Zaiger's varieties in the U.S. The non-Zaiger developed varieties are variously available as well as variously adaptable to USDA hardiness zones. The plants (ultimately trees) of each of these types are, in the main, not unlike their *Prunus* parents, grown on the hardiest parental rootstock, and offering graceful habits, pretty spring blossoms, and variable self-fertility, with each type making its own climatic demands. My advice would be to go to your local fruit tree nursery or online and have a sniff around. And, certainly, if any of these tasty fruits show up in your local supermarket, grab a couple and savor for yourself the fresh flavor excitements this new generation holds.

🪷 65. Pomegranate 'Nana' 🪷
Punica granatum

"Thy lips are like a thread of scarlet, and thy speech is comely; thy temples are like a piece of a pomegranate within thy locks."

—Song of Solomon 4:3

Taxonomists believe that man first began domesticating the pomegranate sometime in the fourth millennium B.C. in northern Iran and Turkey, archeological remains having been unearthed dating to 3000 B.C. in Jericho. From there, the pomegranate spread into Mesopotamia, Egypt, India, northern Africa, and China, and then onto the Mediterranean Basin, where, like many early imports to Greece and Italy, it was identified as a type of apple,—Carl Linnaeus giving them the designation *Malum puncium*, which translates to "apple of Carthage." The species name *granatum* refers to the many seeds inside this fruit plant's colorful, leathery husk, and it is both this abundance of seeds and the fact that, being 85 percent water, loaded with minerals, and toughly storable, the pomegranate came to symbolize health, fertility, and eternal life across a surprising array of early cultures.

In Buddhist tradition, the pomegranate, along with the citron and peach, was considered the most blessed of fruits, and legend maintained that Buddha cured the demoness Hariti of her child-devouring habit by giving her a pomegranate to consume instead. In Islam, the heavenly paradise depicted in the Koran includes a description of the pomegranate, and Islamic legend holds that every pomegranate contains one seed from paradise. In Greek myth, when Hades abducted Persephone and carried her to the underworld, he made her his eternal queen by tempting her with a pomegranate. And in Christian tradition, the pomegranate is a compelling devotional symbol of resurrection and eternal life, as most clearly evidenced in the mythical tale of the unicorn, in which pomegranate seeds "bleed" from its horn, symbolizing the passion of the Savior;

Pomegranate 'Nana'

once tamed, the unicorn is portrayed as chained to a pomegranate tree, symbolic of the resurrection.

Typically smallish trees (12 to 18 feet) bearing bright red flowers and, later, that gorgeously unique fruit, pomegranates are, unfortunately, only truly hardy to USDA zone 8 and above. Therefore, here I will recommend to you another potable dwarf: the lovely heirloom 'Nana.' First described in 1803, and introduced into culture by the German botanist Christian Persoon in 1806, 'Nana' is a dense shrub growing to about 3 or 4 feet and displaying pretty orange/red trumpet-shaped flowers, followed by the requisite leathery-skinned, lushly colored, if somewhat small-scale fruit. In zones where temperatures rarely fall below 40 degrees, 'Nana' will, in multiples, make a wildly effective floriferous hedge. And in climates with winters that don't plummet below 20 degrees, and when planted against a snug southern wall, 'Nana' will do very nicely as a compact shrub, although summers may not be long enough for her to fruit. Nana's real beauty is her diminutive size, which has made her a favored darling of bonsai aficionados: with judicious pruning, she can be restricted to as little as a foot in height.

The pomegranate was prescribed for all kinds of ailments and afflictions, Dioscorides in his *De Materia Medica* of the first century A.D. recording: ". . . pommegranats are of a pleasant taste and good for ye stomach . . . good for the ulcers that are in ye mouth and in ye Genitalls and in the seate, as also . . . for ye paines of ye eares, and for the griefs in ye nosthrills . . ." Pomegranates also contain no fat, cholesterol, or sodium, and are an excellent source of vitamin C and iron. Perhaps the pomegranate's most popular twentieth-century culinary employment has been in the mixed-drink additive grenadine, which currently commercially consists of nothing but corn sweetener and red dye #40. Therefore, to make the real thing, mix 2 cups of 'Nana' seeds and pulp with 2 cups of sugar, boil to reduce, strain out the seeds, bottle, and retire to the bar.

❧ 66. Prickly Pear 'Burbank' ❧
Opuntia ficus-indica

In North Africa, the prickly pear is the main and sometimes only source of water and fodder for animal herds during times of drought, and is referred to as "the bridge of life."

Archeological evidence from coprolites (fossilized human feces) found in the Hinds Cave in Texas in 1973 suggests that the prickly pear is incredibly antiquely native to the Americas, that the fruit and "pads" of the prickly pear have been part of the human diet for over 9,000, years and that domestication could have taken place as early as 6000 B.C. Also known as the "Cactus pear" and "Indian fig" (*ficus-indica*), the prickly pear was such an important food source in ancient Mexico that, according to Aztec legend, the gods decreed that their capital (now Mexico City) would be built on a site identified by an eagle perched on a prickly pear devouring a serpent: the emblem currently emblazoned on the Mexican flag. The prickly pear entered Europe with Christopher Columbus in 1493 and, by the end of the fifteenth century, the succulent green "pads" of the prickly pear had become a broadly popular seagoing scurvy preventative, which eventually served to distribute them through many arid and semiarid regions of the globe.

The term *Opuntia* was applied to the prickly pear by Karl Linnaeus in 1753, but it was the English herbalist Phillip Miller who ultimately coined *Opuntia ficus-indica* in his *Gardener's Dictionary* of 1768. The prickly pear enjoyed widespread medicinal employment as a poultice for wounds and burns, *Opuntia* sap having much the same properties as aloe vera, and, although nearly 90 percent water by weight, the fruits are rich in vitamin C and a good source of carbohydrates while the "pads" abound with vitamins A and B, calcium, magnesium, iron, and soluble fiber. Recent research on the *Opuntia* family has also revealed 8 essential amino acids, and has demonstrated that *Opuntia* can stabilize blood sugar and is especially effective against type II diabetes.

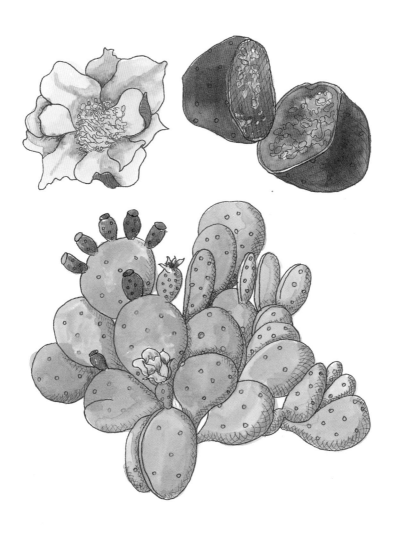

PRICKLY PEAR 'BURBANK'

Tuna is the historic Spanish name for the prickly pear, but today the term *tuna* is popularly applied to its edible fruit. *Nopal* is both the ancient Aztec and modern Mexican and South American word for the prickly pear, but the plural *nopales* is now widely employed in reference to this food plant's fleshy edible "pads." However edible, however, the wild prickly pear consumed by early Americans was of a dramatically "prickly" demeanor, Henri Joutel, post commander of the La Salle Mississippi River Expedition, reporting from Texas in 1687: "One must strip the fruit before eating it because, although the quills are quite small and almost imperceptible, without fail they make one sick . . . One of our soldiers even died from having eaten the fig greedily without wiping it."

It was Luther Burbank who, shortly after the turn of the twentieth century, managed to surmount this culinary stumbling block, ultimately achieving complete spinelessness in the brilliant 'Burbank Thornless.' The 'Burbank Thornless,' hardy only to zones 8 to 10, will make, in about 5 years, a compact, 6-foot mound of 6-inch gray/green *nopales,* each "hinged" to another, first bearing sizeable, bright yellow flowers, followed by large, deep red "pears" (*tunas*) ripening in midsummer. For those of you who can have it in the ground, its preference would be for a sunny position in well-drained sandy loam with some protection from winter winds. For the rest of us, yes, altogether now: "perfect for pot culture!" (I know: those pots may be getting awfully crowded . . .) Sweet, juicy *tunas*, once peeled, may be eaten raw; *nopales* taste somewhat like green beans and are prepared by first peeling, and then cutting or dicing into strips or cubes. A simply splendid, authentically Mexican way to serve the youngest *nopales* ("*nopalitos*") is to grill them until tender and just brown, slice, and toss with a squeeze of lime and a splash of olive oil.

ॐ

67. Quince 'Smyrna'
Cydonia oblonga

"There is no fruit growing in the land that is of so many excellent uses . . . serving as well to make many dishes . . . and much more for their physical virtues."

—John Parkinson, *Paradisi in Sole Paradisus Terrestris*, 1629

The quince is, physically, extremely close to its *Rosaceae* cousins the pear and the apple, different types resembling miniatures of both, and was once even classified as a *Pyrus,* but is now the only species in the genus *Cydonia.* Antiquely native to Persia and Mesopotamia, the Mediterranean quince, *Cydonia oblonga,* oddly, is an entirely different genus from its other relations, the decorative Asian quinces (*Chanomeles speciosa*). Many feel it was the honey-skinned *Cydonia oblonga* that constituted the "golden apples" of Greek myth, legendarily guarded by the Hesperides and spirited away by Hercules, and it is also a popular contender in that whole fruit of Eden mess. We know the Greeks imported improved varieties from Cydon in Crete—thus the derivation of this fruit's botanical name—and dedicated quinces to Aphrodite as symbols of love and fertility.

Columella, in his *De Re Rustica* of the first century A.D., describes three varieties: the "sparrow apple," the "golden apple," and the "must apple," and, in the same century, Pliny the Elder maintained that a quince was capable of warding off "the evil eye." Apicius, author of the world's first cookbook, recommended whole quinces boiled with honey and wine, Charlemagne introduced the quince into France in 812 A.D., and Joan of Arc was known to have received a gift of *cotignac,* a jellied confection made from quince, when she arrived in Orleans in 1429. Wynkyn de Worde, in his English *Boke of Kervynge* of 1509, aside from recommending that one "fruche that chekyn" and "disfygure that pecockes," also glows about "char de Quynce," the antique name for quince marmalade.

QUINCE 'SMYRNA'

In the New World, quince's brief popularity in New England (a March 16, 1629 entry from the Massachusetts Bay Colony requesting quince seed from England) waned quickly as, in colder climates, the fruit, unlike an apple or pear, is inedible raw, and usually with a toughish, fuzzy rind and hard, unpleasant flesh. Therefore, with the advent of more immediately accommodating fruit types, the quince made a quiet exit, and no one seems to grow them anymore, which is why I believe you should. There is absolutely nothing prettier than the gracefully gnarly, sculptural form of a quince tree, and the fruits are excellent when cooked, as well as legendary for their strong, sweet fragrance. Additionally and medicinally, the esteemed seventeenth-century English physician Sir Thomas Browne lauded the quince as "the stomach's comforter," and we know now that quinces are nicely high in vitamins C and B2, potassium, potash, and phosphorus.

Therefore, from the ancient city of Smyrna, Turkey, and imported into North America around the turn of the twentieth century, I bring you the *Cydonia oblonga* 'Smyrna.' Unlike most other quinces, the skin of 'Smyrna's lovely, pear-shaped, golden-ripening fruit, far from being "wooly," is thin and smooth. Growing from 12 to 20 feet, with attractive green foliage turning a superb crimson in fall, 'Smyrna' requires blissfully little care, is readily adaptable to a wide range of soils and temperatures, self-fertile, hardy in zones 5 to 9, and would make a charming addition to any yard. In spring 'Smyrna' will flower with showy pink blossoms resembling an old-fashioned single rose, followed by that famous golden fruit, which, in fall, will unleash that legendarily delicious aroma. As noted, in our precincts, raw quinces are inedible, and are always cooked and sweetened, often into the easiest (and most delicious) of jellies because of their high pectin content: cover washed, cored, and quartered quinces with water in a big pot, boil and mash, strain, add just under a cup of sugar for every cup of juice rendered, reboil till thickened, and jar.

ॐ

68. Raſpberry 'Amity'
❦ 69. Raſpberry 'Fall Gold' ❦
Rubus idaeus

"Twas only to hear the yorling sing,

And pu' the crawflower round the spring,

The scarlet hep and the hindberrie,

And the nut that hang frae the hazel tree."

—Sixteenth-century British verse

Historically and famously, the raspberry has been associated with the two antiquely sacred Mounts Ida, one purportedly their birthplace near the site of the ancient city of Troy in what is now Turkey, the other the highest point on the isle of Crete and, legendarily, boyhood home to Zeus. Consequently, the raspberry was widely known as the "Bramble of Mount Ida" in the Greek *Batos Idaia*, and in the Latin *Rubus Idaea*, which Carl Linnaeus ultimately adopted as its botanical appellation. Raspberry remains have been found in the lake settlements of Switzerland very possibly dating to as long ago as 4000 B.C.; however, there are also both red and black raspberry varieties (*R. strigosus* and *R. occidentalis* respectively) native to North America, and it is supposed that these types were delivered there by travelers or animals crossing the Bering Strait in some equally misty predawn of time. However, oddly, raspberry cultivation is not mentioned anywhere until the writings of Palladius in the fourth century A.D., and then not again until English herbal references of the sixteenth century A.D.

The same scenario seemed to be the case with the native North American types, which were certainly a popular if wild food source for many Native American tribes in our own prehistory. The plain fact is, the raspberry has grown like a prickly topsy in every nation's ditch and hedgerow for so long, no one thought them worth domesticating until a good way along in the history of edible cultivation. The Roman

RASPBERRY 'AMITY'

Raspberry 'Fall Gold'

domestication of raspberries is finally reported by Palladius in his *Opus agriculturae*, and it was the Romans who spread the raspberry throughout Europe, seed remains having been discovered at Roman fort sites in Great Britain. King Edward I, the "Hammer of the Scots," is known to have brought them under cultivation there in the thirteenth century A.D., and, by 1548, the English herbalist John Gerard was glowing about them, calling them "hindberrie," from the ancient Saxon *Hindbeer*.

Rubus ideaus were introduced into the New World with the first English settlers, where they soon commingled rampantly with the native types, producing the antecedents of most of the currently favored varieties. By 1761, George Washington had brought raspberries into cultivation in his gardens at Mount Vernon, and, in 1771, the Prince Nursery of Flushing, New York, listed the first commercially available raspberry plants in the colonies. In 1830, Constantine Samuel Rafinesque, the eccentric nineteenth-century botanist and zoologist (who died a pauper in a Philadelphia attic in 1840 and was posthumously honored with the genus *Rafinesquia*), reported that there were more than 25 wild species, and by 1867, over 40 different varieties of raspberries had been brought into culture, among them red, black, and golden types.

Raspberries have also had a long history of medicinal employment, Nicholas Culpeper commenting in his *Herball* of 1653 that "the fruit has a pleasant grateful smell and taste, is cordial and strengthens the stomach, stays vomiting and good to prevent miscarriage." Native Americans employed a tisane extracted from boiled raspberry leaves to treat pregnancy-related ailments, and it is still most commonly the leaves, brewed into tea, that are employed herbally for expectant mothers during the last weeks of pregnancy to prevent miscarriage, relieve morning sickness, and reduce labor pains, but also for diarrhea, stomach upset, lung congestion, sore throat, and as a wash for wounds and ulcers. It is also known that the Chippewa and Omaha tribes employed a decoction of the roots to treat dysentary and diarrhea, and the Appalachia a root tea for hemorrhaging and hemophilia. Additionally, the usually deeply hued raspberry is a significant source of both anthocyanins and ellagic acid, an important phytonutrient that neutralizes free radicals.

Most currently popular raspberries are offspring of both the Eurasian (*R. ideaus*) and the North American red raspberry (*R. strigosus*), the first lending finer taste, the latter hardiness and adaptability. In this chapter, I am thrilled to introduce you to two of the finest, one red and one yellow, which will make a very pretty dish of berries indeed. The first, the red 'Amity' raspberry, was developed at the Oregon Agricultural Experiment Station in Corvallis, Oregon, in 1984, supplanting the commercially popular variety 'Heritage' in home gardens due to superior adaptability to heavy soils and improved resistance to root rot and aphids. 'Amity' will reward you with large, firm, deep red berries with a "classic" raspberry flavor, equally commendable for fresh eating, freezing, or canning. Additionally, like all raspberries, 'Amity' is self-fertile, hardy in USDA zones 3 through 9, and is one of the "ever-bearing" or "fall-bearing" varieties, meaning it will potentially grace you with two crops per season. And, like all raspberries, beyond a bit of summer weeding, they're as tough as pig iron.

Another "ever-bearing" type, 'Fall Gold' is a relatively modern hybrid hailing from the mountains of Korea, and is notable for both its superb fruit and sturdy habit. Extremely sweet, conical-shaped, golden-blushed-with-pink berries, splendid for both fresh consumption or processing, 'Fall Gold' berries are borne on vigorously erect canes, so these plants will not need support except in very windy situations. By the way, let's get this "ever" and "fall-bearing" thing straight: you can have either. An "ever-bearing" habit is encouraged by cutting back all second-year canes (*floracanes*) to about an inch above ground and shortening all first-year canes (*primocanes*) to 2 feet in fall. This will result in a small spring crop on the bottom of next year's *floracanes*, and an impressive fall crop on the tops of the new *primocanes*. Alternately, you can treat an "ever-bearing" variety as a single-crop "fall-bearing" type by cutting back all canes and allowing new *primocanes* alone to grow in spring for a very prolific autumnal harvest.

Members of the greater *Rubus* family are, technically, not berries at all, but "aggregate fruits," i.e., clusters of "drupelets," each tiny drupelet containing one seed and growing over a fleshy center core, called the "receptacle." When picked, the raspberry's drupelet cluster will detach from the receptacle, so that the "berry" has a cavity at the center, unlike a blackberry, which will detach from the plant with the receptacle intact. Therefore, the black raspberry is a raspberry and the red blackberry is a blackberry, and never the twain shall meet. A very useful thing to do with the harvest of either 'Amity' or 'Fall Gold' would be to put up some raspberry vinegar, an herbal remedy still prescribed for fever, sore throats, and "complaints of the chest," and which, when paired with sparkling or still water, makes a truly superior cooling drink in summer. Therefore, heat 1 1/2 cups white vinegar with 1 cup raspberries and 1/2 cup sugar in a nonreactive pot until fully dissolved and not quite boiling, strain, and bottle. A generous spoonful or two in a tumbler of water will most certainly soothe what ails you.

🎐 70. Rhubarb 'MacDonald' 🎐
Rheum rhabarbarum

"A rhubarb what? A rhubarb tart!

A whatbarb tart? A rhubarb tart!

I want another slice of rhubarb tart!"

—John Cleese, *The Rhubarb Tart Song*, 1968

Rhubarb is a very odd food plant indeed as, for one thing, while its petioles (stalks) are famously edible, its leaves are completely poisonous. For another, until well into the eighteenth century, rhubarb was not considered a food plant at all, but a purely medicinal one. Numbering about 60 species, the most notable *Rheums* are our familiar garden rhubarb (*R. rhabarbarum*), "false" rhubarb (*R. rhaponticum*), and Oriental medicinal rhubarb (*R. officinale*). Some authorities attest *Rheum* derives from the Greek *rheo*, "to flow," in allusion to rhubarb's purgative properties, while the nineteenth-century English botanist John Lindley believed it originated in *Rha*, the ancient name for the Volga River in Russia, on which banks it has grown since man still had gills.

The earliest literary allusion to rhubarb dates to China and 2700 B.C., in reference to the medical applications of *R. officinale*, which successfully assuaged the fever of the Wu emperor of the Liang Dynasty (557–579 A.D.), combated plague during the Song dynasty (960–1127 A.D.), and miraculously cured the Guangzong emperor (1620–1621 A.D.) of the "severe illness" he contracted after having had "a joyful time with four beautiful women." A further point of oddity concerning rhubarb and, specifically, *R. officinale* is the unusual zeal with which all of Europe sought to culture it, only to be abjectly disappointed. It seems that no matter what cultural niceties and varieties were pursued, no plant grown outside of Oriental medicinal rhubarb's native habitat managed to live up to the original, which, of course, made Europe crave it all the more. In fact, in the eighteenth century, the elusive *R. officinale* became such a pan-European obsession, it was remuneratively traded by

RHUBARB 'MacDonald'

the East India Company in mind-boggling quantity, and, in the same century, being native to the Bosphorus, becoming a fantastically profitable Russian state monopoly.

Some type of rhubarb is recorded in Italy by 1608, by 1640 it had spread into northern Europe, and, by 1777, cultivation of *R. rhaponticum* in particular had commenced in Banbury, England, with seed procured from Russia. An unidentified Maine gardener seems to have carried rhubarb into America sometime between 1790 and 1800, and, by 1822, rhubarbs of several descriptions were available in markets, although it was around this period that the culinary possibilities of this primeval-looking food plant had begun to outweigh the medicinal. Therefore, here we will leap the fence to embrace the familiar edible "garden-variety" rhubarb *R. rhabarbarum*, and, more particularly, the popular modern cultivar 'MacDonald.' Also known as 'Macdonald's Canadian Red,' I commend 'MacDonald' to you as being the most commonly available type, for possessing an extremely vigorous, upright habit, and for producing large, tender, red-blushed stalks. Additionally, 'MacDonald' shows fine resistance to wilt and root rot and is hardy to USDA zones 4 to 8.

In spring, in the proper environment, each perennial 'MacDonald' corm will sprout a handsome crown of stout pink to red petioles, every stalk capped with a large, frilly, if sadly poisonous green leaf, and, once planted, 'MacDonald' will remain nicely productive for 8 to 15 years. You will think me ill-natured if I end this chapter with anything but an old-fashioned rhubarb tart recipe. Therefore, dissolve 1 cup of sugar in 1/3 cup of water, add some strips of lemon peel, a broken cinnamon stick, and 6 cups of trimmed, sliced 'MacDonald' rhubarb stalks, bring to a boil, reduce heat, cover, and simmer until rhubarb softens (about 5 minutes). Remove from heat, let cool, and arrange the rhubarb bits in a tart shell brushed with apricot jam. Strain the liquid, boil until reduced to 1/4 cup, cool again, spoon over the rhubarb, and serve with fresh whipped cream.

🎋 71. Sea Buckthorn 🎋
Hippophae rhamnoides

According to Greek legend, the mythical flying horse Pegasus, equine spawn of the sea god Poseidon and the Gorgon Medusa, preferred the leaves of the sea buckthorn to all other foods.

T he widely unknown sea buckthorn's health-giving properties are so astonishing, it would be fairly impossible to recommend a worthier edible or herbal plant for our current millennium, so do listen carefully. A member of the greater *Elaeagnaceae* family, this fascinating food plant most probably originated in prehistory in the foothills of the Altai Mountains of southern Siberia; however, the sea buckthorn also grows seemingly wild at elevations of 14,000 feet in the Himalayas, and along the sandy sea coasts of England, France, Sweden, Denmark, and Germany. Legend holds that the ancient Greeks fed the leaves of the sea buckthorn to their racehorses to improve the gloss of their coats, thus giving birth to its botanical appellation *Hippophae* or "shiny horse." Another ancient tale maintained that, due to its famous salvelike properties, sea buckthorn oil was unadvisable for the boiling "alive" of one's enemies, as they might potentially survive.

In the eighth century A.D., the *Sibu Yidain*, the most authoritative Tibetan medical text in existence, devoted an amazing 30 of its 156 chapters to the sea buckthorn, reporting that it both "tonifies *yin* and strengthens *yang*." The fruit and juice were also favored tonics of Ghengis Khan (1162–1227), whose interior fortification allowed him to live by these words: "The greatest joy a man can know is to conquer his enemies and drive them before him . . . To see the faces of those who were dear to them bedewed with tears, and to clasp their wives and daughters in his arms." Quite a guy. However, sometime during the Middle Ages, the sea buckthorn fell into nearly total obscurity on the European continent, and, astoundingly, was not introduced into the New World until it was carried to the United States by Russian immigrants in the 1920s. There are

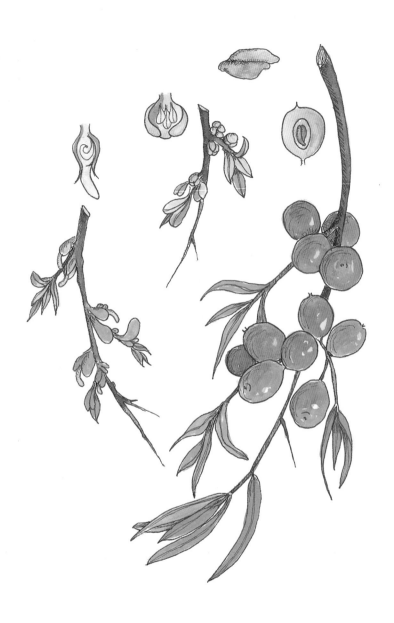

SEA BUCKTHORN

two probable reasons for this: one, the fruit, actually a "nut," is small and acidic, and, two, they are borne on thorny branches so unfriendly, sea buckthorns, like brambles, were anciently grown as protective hedges.

That said, everyone should have some. First of all, they are lovely, small, shrubby trees with silvery gray, willowlike foliage, small yellow flowers preceding leaves in spring, and striking orange/yellow fruit, about the size of a blueberry, growing all along the thorny branches in fall. Secondly, a like weight of sea buckthorn berries contains 9 times as much vitamin C as an orange, plus impressive doses of vitamins A, B, and E, beta-carotene, flavonoids, and both palmitoleic and linoleic acid. This not only adds up to practically unparalleled antioxidant performance, but also extraordinary potential in the fields of cancer therapy, cardio-vascular disease, gastrointestinal ulcers, and cirrhosis of the liver. Additionally, as a topical ointment, sea buckthorn oil is widely prescribed for skin regeneration and healing for those suffering from eczema, burns, wounds and scars, and sun damage.

The sea buckthorn, growing from 6 to 13 feet, depending on soil type, is also an astoundingly hardy (-45 to 103 degrees F), undemanding plant, requiring only good sunlight, and will even lend good health to your soil by reaffixing nitrogen there. The trees are dioecious (either male or female) and, therefore, you will need to plant a small grove of approximately 3 females to 1 male for adequate pollination, and, of course, only the females will produce fruit, about 3 to 5 years from planting. I suggest mixing up both some skin-soothing salve (smash and drain the berries, food process with 2 parts olive oil to 3 parts pulp, let rest, skim off the top layer of oil, and store), as well as a dramatically sustaining beverage (blend fresh, strained juice with equal amounts water and apple juice). *Santé!*

72. Serviceberry (Juneberry)
'Princess Diana'
Amelanchier x *grandiflora*

The pioneers of the Great Plains chose the blossoms of the "service-
berry" to decorate their "services" and graves, as the beautiful
blooms coincided with spring thaw, meaning those who had died over
the winter could finally be buried.

T**he serviceberry, also known variously as the juneberry, shadblow, saskatoon, swamp pear, and western shadbush, is a close-
knit clan of about 25 small deciduous trees and largish shrubs in
the family *Rosaceae*, ranging latitudinally across the North American continent from Newfoundland to the Gulf of Mexico, and with one variety
each in Asia and Europe. *Amelanchier alnifolia* is the species from which
most modern fruiting cultivars are derived, but other notable American
types include *A. arborea*, the downy serviceberry, *A. canadensis*, the shadblow serviceberry, and *A. laevis*, the Allegheny serviceberry.
"Juneberry" is referential to the month in which this lovely tree typically fruits, the designation *Amelanchier* derives from the French *amelanche*
for the European serviceberry, *A. ovalis*, and "shadblow" or "shadbush"
from the fact that this genus's notably beautiful flowers appear when the
shad are running in early spring.

The fact that dried serviceberries were used historically as an important article of trade showcases the unusually high regard Native
Americans displayed toward this, I believe, greatly underappreciated
indigenous food plant. Much like the cranberry, the service berry was
employed by Native Americans, particularly of the Great Plains, in a wide
variety of soups, stews, and sauces, as well as pounded into dried venison
in the preparation of their famous pemmican. The Iroquois and Blackfoot
nations also consumed serviceberries as a laxative, treatment for the liver,
and to regain strength after childbirth; the inner bark of the tree was

SERVICEBERRY (JUNEBERRY) 'PRINCESS DIANA'

chewed or boiled into tea as a remedy for diarrhea, and the wood, being extraordinarily hard, strong, and densely grained, was utilized by legions of Native American warriors to make fine, straight-flying arrow shafts.

George Washington planted several varieties of the serviceberry at Mount Vernon, and another was carried into England in the eighteenth century to be grown as an entrancing exotic by the duke of Argyll. In 1878, the first variety of Native American serviceberry, an *A. alnifolia* type, was selected from the wild, brought into culture, and offered for sale under the prophetic name of 'Success.' The 'Princess Diana' serviceberry (for some reason usually identified as a "juneberry") is one of the "apple" serviceberry types (*Amelanchier* x *grandiflora*), a spontaneous hybrid of the downy serviceberry (*A. arborea*) and the Allegheny serviceberry (*A. laevis*), and so named for the rich "apple red" hue of their leaves in autumn. A Wisconsin-bred royal, introduced to her adoring fans in 1987, 'Princess Diana' garners additional accolades by flowering more prolifically than either of her parents, and offering fruit that is both larger and more succulent, as well as a "trunking" habit, which is a decided improvement over the tendency to sucker in her pedigree.

Typically growing from 15 to 25 feet tall, this regal, willowy, aptly named beauty boasts copious racemes of stunning, starlike white flowers in spring; finely toothed, oval-shaped, bluish/green leaves, which will turn to "apple" crimson in fall; and abundant crops of green berries that will first turn red, and then finally to a deep, succulently sweet-tasting black/purple in early summer. This easygoing royal is also blissfully tolerant to a wide range of soils, and will do splendidly in full sun or part shade and from USDA zone 3b to 8a, all of which attributes should make 'Princess Diana' a must-have for most of you, which is a very fine thing indeed. If you have never tasted a serviceberry, you are in for a treat. Their blueberry-like goodness makes them excellent fresh as well as perfect for jams and pies. However, why not try a pint of these in your favorite blueberry muffin recipe for a nicely sweet change of pace?

❦ 73. Strawberry 'EarliGlow' ❦
74. Strawberry 'Tristar'

Fragaria ananassa

"Doubtless God could have made a better berry, but doubtless God never did."

—Dr. William Butler (1536–1617)

The wild strawberry is anciently native to everywhere save Africa, Australia, and New Zealand. Like the fig, the strawberry is a certifiable fruit oddity, as it is not really a "berry" or even "fruit" at all, but an "aggregate fruit," meaning that what we take to be the "berry" is actually just an extraordinarily tasty, fleshy receptacle and the "fruit," correctly "achenes," are multiply attached to the exterior of it and are what we mistakenly identify as the strawberry's "seeds." The first rather ominous mention of the strawberry in literature seems to take place in Virgil's *Third Ecologue* of about 40 B.C., in which the shepherd Damoetas is warned: "Ye boys that gather flowers and strawberries, Lo, hid within the grass an adder lies." Ovid gives the strawberry a merrier mention in his description of the Golden Age from his epic *Metamorphoses* of 9 A.D.: "The teeming Earth, yet guiltless of the plough, And unprovok'd, did fruitful stores allow: Content with food, which Nature freely bred, On wildings and on strawberries they fed . . ."

The ancient Romans believed wild strawberries could cure everything from bouts of fainting, inflammations, fevers, and halitosis, to all diseases of the blood, liver, and spleen, and, due to its heartlike shape and crimson color, the strawberry was historically associated with Venus and viewed as a powerful aphrodisiac. Oddly, and perhaps again for its heart shape, the strawberry also broadly symbolized "perfection" and "righteousness" in ancient Europe, and many medieval churches display strawberry motifs in their decoration. By the fourteenth century, the tiny wood strawberry (*Fragaria vesca*) had been brought into cultivation in

STRAWBERRY 'EarliGlow'

France, although it was apparently coveted more for the ornament of its flowers than for its edible fruit. In 1368, the French king Charles V ordered 1,200 strawberry plants to be planted into the gardens of the Louvre in Paris and, in 1375, the duke of Burgundy had four full blocks of his *potager* near Dijon dedicated to strawberries.

However, in most societies, people seemed to be entirely delighted with the native, wild, small-fruited varieties that nature offered up to them, Thomas Hyll, author of the first English gardening book, reporting in his *Gardener's Labyrinth* of 1593 that they were "much eaten at all men's tables in the sommer time with wine and sugar," and very little if any real selection occurred. By the end of the sixteenth century, however, one finally hears fairly broad reference to cultivation as physicians discovered, debated, and ultimately lauded the healthful strawberry's mainly spurious medicinal applications. The French *Grete Herball* of 1526 reported: "Fragaria is an herbe called strabery . . . It is pryncypally good agaynst all evylles of the mylt. The uice therof drunken with hony profyteth mervaylously."

In the mid-seventeenth century, Roger Williams, founder of Rhode Island, marveled at New England's amazing abundance of wild strawberries, observing, "I have many times seen as many as would fill a good ship," and America's first great horticulturist William Bartram wrote of strawberry fields so vast and plentiful that they dyed the legs of his horses as they rode through, and rather voyeuristically reported from North Carolina in 1776 that "companies of young, innocent Cherokee virgins . . . were yet collecting strawberries or wantonly chasing their companions, tantalizing them, staining their lips and cheeks with the rich fruit." It was the importation of the native American strawberry (*Fragaria virginiana*) into Europe in the seventeenth century, and then the introduction of the 'Chili' strawberry (*Fragaria chiloensis*) in the eighteenth century that would finally spark the development of the voluptuously fruited varieties we know today.

It is believed to be Thomas Hariot, Sir Walter Raleigh's scientific adviser, who first relayed the 'Virginia' strawberry to England in 1585, and there is clear evidence that the first Chilean strawberry was delivered into France in 1714, when the French spy Amedée François Frézier carried them home from South America. In 1759, Philip Miller, director of the Chelsea Physics Garden in London, described a large fruiting strawberry obtained from George Clifford, director of the Netherlands East India Company, and most taxonomists now identify the 'Miller' strawberry as the first cultivated offspring of the Virginia strawberry and the 'Chili.' Called "Pineapple" or "Pine" strawberries (*Fragaria ananassa*), as their scent was thought to resemble that of a pineapple (thus *ananassa*), these late-eighteenth-century cultivars are the antecedents of all modern cultured varieties.

There are two basic subsets of the modern strawberry, their division based on fruiting and flowering: the "June-bearing" types, requiring short days, cool temperatures, and bearing fruit only in spring, and the "ever-bearing" varieties, which, as the name would suggest, yield fruit throughout the growing season. Here I will stop to acquaint you with a stellar variety of each. The June-bearing 'EarliGlow,' a relative ingénue on the strawberry stage, is a true showstopper for its phenomenal climatic adaptability, shining from Maine right down to the Carolinas (USDA zones 4 to 8). Developed by the U.S. Department of Agriculture, this new darling's trademarks seem to be fantastic flavor, color, vigor, and disease resistance, many considering bright crimson, medium-sized, nicely firm fruit of the 'EarliGlow' to be the best flavored of all June-bearing varieties. Additionally, they "pick" earlier and hold size longer than most other early fruiting types, and, if all that is not sufficient luster, in research done at Cornell University in 2003, 'EarliGlow' proved to be an antioxidant colossus, being rated tops in cancer cell proliferation inhibition and nearly twice as high in total antioxidant activity as the next contender.

Of the "ever-bearings," it is the 'Tristar' variety that seems to be the currently reigning darling for the triple threat of reliable production, excellent flavor, and superior resistance to hot temperatures (up to 95 degrees) as well as *red stele* and *verticillium* wilt. The first year of planting, expect 'Tristar' to provide you with an impressive fall crop of brilliant red berries, and then, for the next 3 seasons, you can rely on a notable spring harvest, followed by five or six additional flushes right through to September. Like all strawberries, 'Tristar' is a treasure trove

Strawberry 'Tristar'

of nutrition, containing both ellagic acid, which is powerfully antioxidant, and flavonoids, which help keep "bad" cholesterol from oxidizing, and a single cup will deliver an astonishing 140 percent of your daily dose of vitamin C.

Culturally, both 'EarliGlow' and 'Tristar' plants, with their lush greenery, pretty white, yellow-eyed flowers, and lovely ruby fruit, should be set about a foot apart in a sandy to loamy soil with good drainage and a pH of 5 to 7, and then allowed to fill in by pinching off the flowers in the first season in order to encourage the production of runners. Plants may then be fruited for 2 or 3 seasons following establishment, and then renovated in the fourth year when fruit quality and yield start to wane. A good mulching in winter will also increase your chances of success. For these scrumptious berries, I say pick a pint, slice and toss with a bit of sugar and lemon juice, and did someone say "shortcake"?

🌿 75. Wolfberry (Goji) 🌿
Lycium barbarum

Goji berry legend holds that, one day, a traveling merchant, who beheld a young woman whipping an ancient gentleman, asked: "Why are you assaulting this old man?" The lady replied, "I am disciplining my great-grandson."

Although its origins are murky (probably southern Eurasia), the *Lycium barbarum* has been employed in Traditional Chinese Medicine for as long as recorded history. The young woman described above proved to be 300 years old and, when asked the source of her miraculous youth, she replied that the herb had many names and an application for every season: "In spring, take its leaves, known as 'essence of heaven' . . . In the summer, its flowers, known as 'longevity of life.' In the autumn, its fruits, known as 'goji berry.' In the winter, the bark of its roots, known as 'the skin and bone of the earth' . . . Take these four parts in the four seasons and you will have a life as lofty as heaven and earth." Historically, the goji is also linked to the legendary emperor Shen Nung, father of Chinese agriculture and medicine, and to the potentially mythical Chinese herbal master Li Qing Yuen, who supposedly married 14 times, lived to the age of 252, had 11 generations of descendants at his death, and was known to consume goji berries daily.

Known equally charmingly as the "Matrimony Vine" in China and the "Duke of Argyll's Tea Tree" in England, the seventh-century Chinese medical text *Yao Xing Lun* further maintained that the "wolf" or "goji" berry could "replenish the supply of body fluids, calm the spirit, refresh the skin, brighten the complexion, and strengthen the eyes," and the *Shi Liao Ben Cao* of the tenth century claimed that it "strengthens the muscles . . . prevents colds, and leads to longevity." Today, botanists tout the amazing goji berry as the most "nutrient-dense substance" known to man, and credit it with everything from reinforcing the immune system and combating fatigue and sexual dysfunction to improving vision, strengthening the liver, regulating blood pressure, and preventing cancer.

What modern science tell us is that gojis contain at least 6 vitamins (including C, B1, and B2), 18 amino acids, 11 essential minerals (including zinc, iron, copper, and calcium), 22 trace minerals, dozens of phytochemicals (including carotenoids, phenolics, and lycopene), and that, in 2005, the goji's "Oxygen Radical Absorbance Capacity" (ORAC), which scores antioxidancy, received, at 30,300 TEs (micromoles of Trolox Equivalents per 100 grams)—the highest rating of any known food plant. Although further testing is necessary, in a recent Chinese study, a group of elderly patients were given doses of goji for 3 weeks, the highest percentage of them tripling their T-cell transformation functions and doubling the activity of their white cell interleukin-2, a whopping 95 percent showing increased appetite and improved sleep function, and 100 percent demonstrating "significantly increased spirit and optimism."

Additionally, the wolfberry is a hardy, unfussy brute: a thick bush reaching from 8 to 10 feet, withstanding winters down to -15 degrees F and summers above 100 degrees F, adapting to almost any sunny situation, and potentially thriving for several hundred years. In early summer, this unbelievably healthful food plant is laden with tiny, trumpet-shaped, purple and white flowers, followed in late summer by glossy, bright crimson gojis, and it will continue to both flower and produce fruit right up until heavy frost. Honestly, fresh gojis are of variable savor, dependent on climate and soil, are difficult to harvest as they are notably easily bruised and are, historically, shaken gently into trays, and then slow-dried in the shade. For this reason, gojis are almost always found dried outside of their production regions, tasting much like raisins or dried cranberries, and are plentiful in health food stores, as are several varieties of goji juice drinks. My advice? Plant one, buy some, go forward—and prosper.

ॐ

WOLFBERRY (GOJI)

❧ Bibliography ❧

A Garden of Pleasant Flowers
(*Paradisi in Sole Paradisus Terrestris*)
John Parkinson
Dover Publications 1976

A Modern Herbal
Mrs. M. Greive
Dover Publications 1982

Bob Flowerdew's Complete Fruit Book
Bob Flowerdew
Kyle Cathie Limited 1997

Cornucopia: The Lore of Fruits & Vegetables
Annie Lise Roberts
Knickerbocker Press 1998

Culpeper's British Herbal
Nicholas Culpeper
W. Foulsham & Co., Ltd.

Enquiry Into Plants
Volumes 1 & 2
Theophrastus
Harvard University Press 1916

Fruit and Vegetables from Seed
Richard Gorer
Webb & Bower 1982

Gerard's Herbal
John Gerard
Spring Books 1927

Growing Unusual Fruit
Alan E. Simmons
Walker & Company 1972

Herbal Simples
W. T. Fernie, M.D.
John Wright & Sons Ltd. 1914

Rhind's Vegetable Kingdom
William Rhind
Blackie & Son 1857

The Backyard Berry Book
Stella Otto
OttoGraphics 1995

The Backyard Orchardist
Stella Otto
OttoGraphics 1993

The Berry Growers Companion
Barbara L. Bowling
Timber Press 2000

The Folk-Lore of Plants
T. F. Thiselton Dyer
Llanerch Publishers 1994

The Origins of Fruit & Vegetables
Jonathan Roberts
Universe Publishing 2001

The Vegetable, Fruit & Nut Book
Barbara Friedlander
Grosset & Dunlap 1974

Thomas Jefferson's Garden Book
Thomas Jefferson
The American Philosophical Society 1944

Thornton's Herbal
Robert John Thornton, M.D.
B. & R. Crosby & Co. 1814

Uncommon Fruits for Every Garden
Lee Reich
Timber Press 2004

Wyman's Gardening Encyclopedia
Donald Wyman
MacMillan Publishing 1971

❧ Resources ❧

ag.arizona.edu
botanical.com
davesgarden.com
ealdriht.org
ediblelandscaping.com
egreenway.com
gallowglass.org
gardendigest.com
hcs.osu.edu
hort.purdue.edu
lib.uchicago.edu
magicspells.in.com
manataka.org
onegreenworld.com
oregon-berries.com
oregonstate.edu
quotegarden.com
raintreenursery.com
taes-weslaco.net
tarahill.com
tytynursery.com
uga.edu
uwm.edu
weeksberry.com
wikipedia.com